God at the End of the Century

GOD AT THE END OF THE CENTURY

David Spriggs

BRITISH AND FOREIGN BIBLE SOCIETY
Stonehill Green, Westlea, Swindon, SN5 7DG, England

A catalogue record for this book is available from the British Library
ISBN 0564 088951

Typeset by BFBS Production Services Department (TP Section)
Printed in Great Britain by Biddles Ltd, Guildford
Cover design by Litchfield Morris, Gloucester
Illustrations by Mike Dilly

Bible Societies exist to provide resources for Bible distribution and use. The
British and Foreign Bible Society (BFBS) is a member of the United Bible
Societies, an international partnership working in over 180 countries. Their
common aim is to reach all people with the Bible, or some part of it, in a
language they can understand and at a price they can afford. Parts of the Bible
have now been translated into over 2,000 languages. Bible Societies aim to
help every church at every point where it uses the Bible. You are invited to
share in this work by your prayers and gifts. The Bible Society in your
country will be very happy to provide details of its activity.

CONTENTS

Dedication

Preface   i

1   Convictions   1

2   A personal journey   11

3   The biblical basis   22

4   Why bother?   38

DEVELOPING OUR AWARENESS OF GOD

5   Christian meditation – an introduction   48

6   Interaction and imagination   61

7   Looking around   77

8   Looking inwards   88

9   Looking backwards   96

10   Looking outwards   111

11   Looking away   121

12   Looking, hear, and there!   134

13   Looking now   145

14   Enriching our faith   161

15   Conclusion   177

DEDICATION

Anyone reading this book will soon discover I am indebted to almost everyone whose life has had contact with mine, for in some ways this book is an aspect of me!

But, there are some people who have been involved more directly. My thanks are due to Simon Reynolds at Bible Society for his patience; to Carl, and especially Mary, at the Evangelical Alliance who have worked hard to produce a manuscript; to Ruth who helped me with some important fine-tuning; to Hazel who, several years ago, shared the leadership with me of an amazing Coventry Christian Training Programme course 'Open to God'. So, it is above all to God that the dedication of this book is due, for if it is of any consequence it is because this book is about an aspect of God's relationship with us.

PREFACE

This book is written from a passionate conviction. Not only is there a God, revealed to us through Jesus Christ, but he is a God infinitely worth knowing. More important and amazing still God wants us to know him, not as some kind of object but as a friend.

> *All this is done by God who, through Christ, changed us from enemies into his friends and gave us the task of making others his friends also.*

2 Corinthians 5.18

Moreover, this God is the same God who created and sustains the universe, and he desires us to know him inwardly and intimately.

> *The God who said, "Out of darkness the light shall shine", is the same God who made his light shine in our hearts, to bring us the knowledge of God's glory shining in the face of Christ.*

2 Corinthians 4.6

This book, then, is about helping us experience and enjoy his light shining in our hearts. As such it owes a great deal to those who have practised and written about Christian Meditation previously.

So, what is Christian Meditation?

Campbell McAlphine describes it in this way.

> *Meditation is the practice of pondering, considering and reflecting on verses of Scripture in total dependence on the Holy Spirit to give revelation of truth and meaning, and by obedient response and reception of that Word, having it imparted to the inner being... Meditation is inwardly receiving truth.* [1]

Brother Ramon SSF, although from a very different tradition and using different language, is saying very similar things when he writes:

> *Meditation implies and necessitates the function of the mind and the use of the imagination with the disciplined constraints of the facts of the text, within the common understanding of the Church... Meditation is that function of the mind and heart whereby you go beyond the word of Scripture and enter into its very heart.* [2]

Nancy Goudie, in a rather racier style, puts it in this way:

> *What is meditation? It sounds dodgy, doesn't it? – like*
> *something out of an Eastern religion!... It's completely*
> *biblical! There are many references regarding meditation*
> *in the Bible... Transcendental Meditation tells you to empty*
> *your mind – Christian Meditation is allowing God and*
> *Scripture to fill your mind.*[3]

In applying this to Scripture she indicates these steps (following Alex Buchanan):

> *Look up Romans 8.1*
> *Ask God to speak to you through it.*
> *Read it through several times.*
> *Spend time thinking about what it says – allow the words to be*
> *absorbed into your mind.*
> *Perhaps dwell on a phrase or section of the verse.*
> *Allow yourself to follow a train of thought until you see*
> *something in the verse you've never seen before.*[4]

Clearly there are two main components common to these approaches to meditation. First there is the focus of the meditative process, i.e. the Scriptures, because in them Christians believe God has revealed himself in a very special way. Secondly there is an approach, variously described as "reflecting", "total dependence", "imparted to the inner being", "inwardly receiving truth", "go beyond the word", "allowing God and Scripture to fill your mind", "use of the imagination", "enter its very heart", "absorbing into your mind".

There is a third point, however, which is a concern to relate this approach to reality to God's revelation. It is not some kind of totally subjective fantasy, but there is also a clear sense that the truth received in this way is more than intellectual knowledge.

For me, biblical meditation is a very significant component of Christian Meditation, but it is not its totality. Why? Because part of our Christian faith is that God reveals himself through his creation as the God who says "Let Light shine out of darkness" and through human beings in particular.

So, we can take the approach but apply it also to different focuses. We also need to take on board the concern, and find ways of ensuring that our more inward and intimate awareness of God, which comes when we "go beyond" objects, situations and people, and "enter their very heart", remains true to God's real nature.

So we need to ask God to speak to us through our world (which is also his), to be willing to spend time looking and listening with a new kind of openness, integrating our imaginations with our minds, dwelling on what we sense, allowing ourselves to "follow a train of thought" until we see something we have never seen before. As we seek to be "Open to God", we shall find he is a "God of Surprises".[5] To borrow a phrase from another author, this book is about becoming aware of our "unattended moments", described by the author as "brief flashes of experience... epiphanies of another order of reality... unattended in the sense that they do not seem to fit into our ordinary patterns of experience".[6] They are, then, the moments when eternity breaks through to us, within the every day; they are the truly significant meaning of our ordinary awareness.

If this sounds remote and highbrow, then I apologize, for part of my passionate conviction is that such awareness of God is meant for each and every Christian, and God desires it for all human beings.

So, this is how I would describe Christian Meditation. It is the attempt to develop a personal, inward relationship with God, through a consciously developed awareness of his reality in Scripture, people, and the world of nature and technology.

It is based on the assumption that God wishes to share himself with us and that we can experience this not only with our minds but through our whole personality. On our part there is a need for alert openness, a willingness to receive from him, however and whenever in his sovereignty he chooses to meet with us.

This book concentrates on God's availability to us, through people and technology, especially the latter, partly because these focuses have received less attention, and partly because they are constantly available to most of us in our ordinary routine lives. One of the Bible's favourite metaphors for humanity's relationship with God is "walking" – the ordinary, regular way of going on

Walking was the normal way of getting around for ordinary people, when there was no emergency. Its use reinforces the validity of the concerns of this book, to discover what God is saying in and through our everyday lives.

The rest of this book is my attempt to help you discover what you may already sense, to introduce approaches which may take you further into the relationship with God, in whom we live and move and have our being. It can be divided roughly into two parts. The first four chapters are foundational; they are not written as a progression, but like the four sides of the foundations of a house – they provide the platform on which the rest is built. In them I share my conviction that

God is to be found in our modern technological urban world and I reveal some of the highlights of my own discovery. Next we look at some aspects of the biblical basis for this approach, which is a very important issue, and then I indicate some of the values which Christian Meditation can bring. The second part begins with chapter 5, where we start to break into the experience of Christian Meditation by examining the personal reality of a very mundane experience. This is to show that the scientifically observable is not the whole of the reality in any situation. Then we begin to sensitize ourselves so as to create the ability to enter "the very heart" of things using some well-tried meditation approaches.

From now on we are moving into less well–charted waters. This is where we come face to face with our real aim of finding out how we can relate personally to God in and through our world to the end of this twentieth century. This is the more exciting, exploratory part of the book, where I share with you some of the amazing moments I have enjoyed with God as he has met me. I do this not to boast (it is totally through his grace and sovereignty), but to encourage you to "look" beyond the surface of your life and your environment to discover more of who God is with you.

So, I invite you now to enter the banqueting hall and let the feast begin.

> *Lord, overshadow me with Thy Spirit,*
> *Banish distraction, inattention, coldness;*
> *Make mine eyes to see, mine ears to hear,*
> *my tongue to speak, my soul to be still;*
> *And then be merciful to my prayer,*
> *and to me a sinner;*
> *for Christ's sake.*

Notes

1   *The Practice of Biblical Meditation* (London, 1986), p. 81.

2   *Praying the Bible* (London, 1988) (Christian Spirituality Series), p. 33.

3   *Developing Spiritual Wholeness* (Word (UK) Ltd, 1993), pp. 53, 54.

4   Ibid., p. 54.

5   See also the book of the same name by G. W. Hughes, London, 1987.

6   Michael Paffard, *The Unattended Moment* (London, 1976).
     Michael Paffard acknowledges his dependence on T. S. Eliot's
     The Four Quartets – perhaps Eliot has the best summary
     "the moment in and out of time".

1 CONVICTIONS

Lord, you have examined me and you know me,
You know everything I do;
  from far away you understand all my thoughts.
You see me whether I am working or resting;
  you know all my actions.
Even before I speak,
  you already know what I will say.
You are all around me on every side;
  you protect me with your power.
Your knowledge of me is too deep;
  it is beyond my understanding.

Where could I go to escape from you?
Where could I get away from your presence?
If I went up to heaven, you would be there;
  if I lay down in the world of the dead
  you would be there.

If I flew away beyond the east
  or lived in the farthest place in the west,
you would be there to lead me,
  you would be there to help me,
I could ask the darkness to hide me
  or the light round me to turn into night,
but even darkness is not dark for you,
  and the night is as bright as the day.
  Darkness and light are the same to you.

You created every part of me;
  you put me together in my mother's womb.
I praise you because you are to be feared;
  all you do is strange and wonderful.
  I know it with all my heart.
When my bones were being formed,
  carefully put together in my mother's womb,
when I was growing there in secret,
  you knew that I was there –
  you saw me before I was born.

The days allotted to me
had all been recorded in your book,
before any of them ever began.
O God, how difficult I find your thoughts;
how many of them there are!
If I counted them, they would be more
than the grains of sand.
When I awake, I am still with you.

O God, how I wish you would kill the wicked!
How I wish violent men would leave me alone!
They say wicked things about you;
they speak evil things against your name.
O Lord, how I hate those who hate you!
How I despise those who rebel against you!
I hate them with a total hatred;
I regard them as my enemies.

Examine me, O God, and know my mind;
test me, and discover my thoughts.
Find out if there is any evil in me
and guide me in the everlasting way.

Psalm 139

And teach them to obey everything I have commanded you.
And I will be with you always, to the end of the age.

Matthew 28.20

And I tell you more: whenever two of you on earth agree
about anything you pray for, it will be done for you by my
Father in heaven. For where two or three come together in
my name, I am there with them.

Matthew 18.19–20

In conclusion, my brothers and sisters, fill your minds with
those things that are good and that deserve praise; things
that are true, noble, right, pure, lovely, and honourable.
Put into practice what you learnt and received from me,
both from my words and from my actions. And the God who
gives us peace will be with you.

Philippians 4.8–9

What amazing certainties. What astounding promises. What absolute commitment. God is so near us, his presence so all embracing. Yet, for many of us it is only too easy to live our busy, pressurized lives with hardly a scent of God's presence.

Of course, most of us would not deny the truth or the relevance of either the promise or the experience of those who live in these truths. But for many Christians today there is a gap, varying from large to enormous between the truth that God is here, now, and our living experiential awareness of Him or his felt absence. Like one of the psalmists we long for God, like the deer driven on by fear of death as the hunters pursue it. We are equally desperate to catch the breath of God to fill our spiritual lungs as the deer is to run on and survive. But so often we gasp in vain or settle for shallow breathing as it proves less painful.

Why are we so unaware of the presence of God? Many answers are supplied today. But not only are there many answers to the questions, there are also many proposed solutions to the problem the question represents. Several of the popular Christian books on how to reawaken our awareness of God's presence are about meditation. Some encourage us to meditate on Scripture, and that is certainly a positive, proper, and helpful thing to do. Scriptural meditation can enhance our awareness of God and should certainly be an important, if not the most important element in any process of meditation. Others help us to "centre down". Perhaps they encourage us to go to some quiet retreat centre, or at least to a specially prepared place of quiet in our home. Others involve visiting the countryside, walking among its quietude and solitude, and absorbing the peace, the gentle harmonies of bird song, the intricate beauty of the flower, the perennial strength and stability of the trees or mountains. Still others will cause us to focus on a candle, with its vulnerability, warm light, and living flame, or some other similar, potentially symbolic object. All of these, and many more processes, can help us recapture our inherit-ance. Like learning to walk again in the physiotherapy department of the hospital, the hope is that we shall gain sufficient attunement in the special place, to sustain us in the ordinary streets of life.

Indeed there is a real value in all these processes and the many others which people with Spirit-given ingenuity devise and demonstrate. We *can* be helped to meditate and become more sensitive to God's presence. I have been helped myself by immersion in such experiences and I know of many more who have also. I delight and rejoice in such growth opportunities.

If I did not firmly believe in the real presence of God in our lives, of his desire for us to live in alert awareness of him, I would not be writing this book. Equally, if I did not believe that we can learn to discern his presence, there would be little point in writing either – for the whole purpose of this book is to help us grow in our daily aware- ness of God, by which I mean our sense of God in and through our ordinary experience.

I am painfully aware of the limitations of the printed page for this purpose. So, too, are many of those who have, in recent years, sought to foster this sense of God in our midst. Hence the word has been supplemented by line drawing, photographs and tape recordings, recognizing that communication is by no means limited to the written work or even the spoken word. Indeed, part of our problem is that we have tended to restrict "divine communication" to that which can be communicated verbally and so have minimized our ability to hear God, see God, find God, meet God, experience God through other forms of communication which impinge on us at deeper, or at least different, levels of awareness. So there has been a re-evaluation of the visual arts, music, sense, smell, and touch as a medium for growth in awareness of God. Yet, however much we stretch the capacity of modern communication techniques there is no substitute for a skilled, insightful, and encouraging person to help us over the fence which hides the glory of the sun from us; up the next slope, whose summit will reveal greater glory; if only we can find the courage and the motivation to reach it. We need someone standing by us who can help our fledgeling awareness stagger on into real flight, who can protect us when emotionally and spiritually we are vulnerable with uncer- tainty, hardly daring to believe that the glimmer of light we see can come from the sun rather than our own candle. We also need someone to protect us from becoming entranced with our own image. This is both the appeal and the danger of the New Age Movement and other new religious movements which encourage *self*-fulfilment and tell us we are gods. We, as Christians, can become so fascinated with the process, so fulfilled by the journey and its endless delights, that we forget the reason for it – to love him more dearly, follow him more nearly every day. A spiritual mentor is a great asset here.

So, why write a book? However poor a substitute for a person beside you, it is written by a person who has struggled, with the help of many others, along the road. More importantly, I have discovered that the Holy Spirit truly is the comforter in the process of discovery. He is the "friend beside us, pleading for us, pleading with us". So we are not as alone as we may think. Hopefully, too, many who use this book will do so with others. In one area one may be a few steps ahead, in a different aspect, someone else may take the lead; thus we can help one another along. In other cases, this book or parts of it may prove useful for those who have the privilege of guiding others. So, fully aware of the limitations of any book as a sufficient tool, especially aware of the limitations of this book for its purposes, I commend you to God as you move on with him.

So, why write *this* book if there are already several excellent helps for us, and if anyway there are ways in which any book is handicapped and limited because of the nature of the quest and the needs of these who seek for help? The short answer is that I consider it a vital and necessary one to help us discover God in our modern, complex urban world.

W. R. Inge was a thoughtful bishop from a previous period. Yet his comments are often perceptive and relevant. He wrote:

> *The modern town dweller has no God and no devil; he lives*
> *without awe, without admiration, without fear.* [1]

If this was true for his times (1860–1945), how much more is that true for us? However, it may well be that it is not only town dwellers who find their normal surroundings unhelpful for discovering God's presence. I have my doubts as to whether visits to the countryside or meditations on sheep in a field would yield half as many insights for those who actually belong to the countryside and for whom sheep are work, as they do for those of us whose visits are enhanced (or should we say "distorted") by nostalgia and romantic ideals. Yet, I know of some whose hands are gnarled by agriculture work and whose skin is toughened by the weathering of the years, who are aware of God in their daily environment and their working world. This however reinforces and does not conflict with my view. My contention is that the urban person's flat, the factory or office context, the noisy, dangerous street, can become the ingredients for insights from God and encounters with God, equally well as the quiet and the rural. The issue of whether it is a rural or urban context is very secondary, although we may need extra help initially to recognize God's presence in the technology of our day.

There are many reasons why I hold this conviction. One is experience and experimentation. In one sense this is a trivial reason and could be dismissed as idiosyncratic, or even personal confusion. In another sense it is important because this is the reason and the motivation for my writing this book. It is because I have discovered that our sometimes sordid and tatty world can be God's home, his hiding place, waiting for us to discover his presence, that I want to help others find him here too. But certainly one person's whim could well become everyone else's wasteland if that is all there was to it. But it is not.

It seems to me that the whole thrust of Scripture is that God reveals his truth and meets with his people, where they are, however mundane or urban that context is. We will spend more time on this issue a couple of chapters hence, but let me illustrate how easily we can be misled. One of today's top ten hymns is "Dear Lord and Father of Mankind". Many find it a beautiful hymn which they sing with deep meaning and relief, even those for whom modern songs have an important place in their spirituality. The whole hymn is full of words which make it appropriate for those who long for a relationship of quality with God.

> *Dear Lord and Father of mankind,*
> *forgive our foolish ways;*
> *re-clothe us in our rightful mind;*
> *in purer lives Thy service find,*
> *in deeper reverence, praise.*
>
> *In simple trust like theirs who heard,*
> *beside the Syrian Sea,*
> *the gracious calling of the Lord,*
> *let us, like them, without a word*
> *rise up and follow Thee.*
>
> *O Sabbath rest by Galilee!*
> *O calm of hills above,*
> *where Jesus knelt to share with Thee*
> *the silence of eternity,*
> *interpreted by love!*
>
> *With that deep hush subduing all,*
> *our words and works that drown,*
> *the tender whisper of Thy call,*
> *as noiseless let Thy blessing fall,*
> *as fell Thy manna down.*
>
> *Drop Thy still dews of quietness,*
> *till all our strivings cease;*
> *take from our souls the strain and stress,*
> *and let our ordered lives confess*
> *the beauty of Thy peace.*

Breathe through the heats of our desire
Thy coolness and Thy balm;
let sense be dumb, let flesh retire;
speak through the earthquake, wind and fire,
O still small voice of calm!

J. G. Whittier, 1807–82

However, an examination of its poetic qualities is revealing. It seems that it strongly enforces our tendency to equate meditation with a kind of escapism. In simple trust, without a word, let us rise up and follow the Lord, who walks beside the Syrian Sea (note not the Galilean Sea, the use of the double sibilant recalls the swish of the waves).

It is sabbath rest, the calm of hills above, the silence of eternity (note not the vibrant clamorous praise of heaven depicted in the Book of Revelation). There is a "deep hush" subduing all speech and activity, for our words and works drown Christ's call. Coping with strain and stress are set in conflict with the beauty of Christ's peace (in contrast to the peace Christ promises in the midst of trouble).

And so we could go on. Almost every phrase, let alone every stanza, of this hymn enhances the current picture and process of meditation as getting away from our world of work, commerce, and activity. This is a hymn I love and one that I have often found helpful as part of preparation for worship. Yet it does seem a strange and strong contrast with some aspects of a robust biblical faith. This is probably best indicated in the last verse.

Breathe through the heats of our desire [2]
Thy coolness and Thy balm.
Let sense be dumb, let flesh retire:
Speak through the earthquake, wind and fire,
O still small voice of calm.

Now, of course, there is a clear reference to the Old Testament incident of Elijah's flight to Mount Carmel (1 Kings 18–19). This is itself apparently a valuable endorsement of the need "to retreat", to get away from the source of conflict and intense activity to be in the wilderness, alone, surrounded by the calling emptiness of nature.

It is a retreat to Horeb, or Mount Sinai, the place of spiritual encounter for a previous generation – the place where Moses was given the law and the people entered into covenant with God. So, it is also an encouragement to go on pilgrimage, to retrace our steps along the pathway to our roots as a brief resumé of the situation will endorse.

After his demanding encounter with the four hundred prophets of Baal, in which God answered Elijah's call to consume the sacrifice by fire from heaven, after the violence of their destruction, cleaning the nation of their evil power, after the strenuous intercession on top of Mount Carmel for the coming of the rains after years of drought, after his Spirit-compelled race to Jezreel, it is not surprising that Elijah needed to retreat to Sinai, to be alone with God. How beautiful and delicate that God was, not in the violence and the noise of howling wind, fearsome earthquake, and awesome fire as he had been previously, but "after the fire, there was the soft whisper of a voice" (1 Kings 19.13).

> *Speak through the earthquake, wind and fire,*
> *O still small voice of calm.*

But all of this probably misses the point of the biblical narrative.[3] If someone was in God's will then he would speak through the earthquake, wind, and fire.

Whittier's poem – its context and his phrase "speak through the earthquake" – how should this be interpreted?

> *The Lord said to Moses, "I will come to you in a thick cloud, so that the people will hear me speaking with you and will believe you from now on".*

> Exodus 19.9, see verses 16–22 and 20.18–21

> *The voice of the Lord is heard on the seas;*
> *the glorious God thunders,*
> *and his voice echoes over the ocean.*

> *The voice of the Lord breaks the cedars,*
> *He makes the mountains of Lebanon jump like calves.*

> *The voice of the Lord makes the lightning flash.*

> Psalm 29.3, 5–7

Clearly God is gracious and not restricted in the way he will communicate with his servant, but equally clearly Elijah is in the wrong place.

> *A voice said to him "Elijah, what are you doing here?"*

> 1 Kings 19.13

God appears to have no truck with Elijah's whingeing reply, and sends him back into the real world of politics, military conflict, and religious rigour, perhaps with the further implication that he has, by his retreat to Sinai, forfeited his right to the prophetic office.

The Lord said, "Return to the wilderness near Damascus, then enter the city and anoint Hazael King of Syria, anoint Jehu son of Nimshi as King of Israel, and anoint Elisha to succeed you as prophet" (1 Kings 19.15–16).

That soft whisper of a voice certainly contained an iron fist of a message! The still small voice was stirring up a hurricane, not establishing a spiritual calm. The last thing this passage is, is an endorsement of our feeling for retreats to the countryside, pilgrimages to our spiritual ancestors' holy ground. It does not suggest that quiet meditation is the only prepared ground into which the seed of God's personal revelation will be liberally scattered.

Now, one incident in Scripture does not destroy the value of meditation and retreat. I certainly have no desire to do that, but because of the power of Whittier's hymn and, it must be said, many sermons on Elijah's flight to Sinai, it is important to check the biblical foundations for the present movements and at least see whether God is not saying something to us about his availability in our modern world of noise and intense activity (words and works).

I have one further thought, which draws me on to share this book with you. If God is not to be found here, in our secular world, we are in trouble, deep trouble, for this is the world of most people most of the time.

Increasingly, as we move towards the end of one century and the beginning of another, our world will be a prefabricated, technologically constructed world – a place where virtual reality threatens to take over from urban reality. Can God not be found in all of this? Well, this book is an attempt to help prepare the way – to seek to throw a line before the distance between drifting ship and secure powered tug becomes too great, and we end up with some giant oil tanker spilling its valuable cargo in a destructive mess because it has been driven by the pressures of modernity on to the jagged rocks of our real world. What a desperate waste – the cargo of our faith is like crude oil; it is a valuable commodity which can propel vehicles of discovery, warm homes of rich humanity, and light dark streets with necessary spiritual protection.

So I am inviting you to take hold of the line this book throws. This is not so that forever you are limited to the routes I can take, but so that in safety you can move onward in your own way, with your own rich commodity, to your own destination.

Before we seek to plan our route, and root ourselves in Scripture, I would like to share a few key factors in my own spiritual pilgrimage.

Notes

1   Outspoken Essays: Our Present Discontents – quoted *Concise Dictionary of Quotations* (London, 1993), p. 251.

2   The hymn is actually part of a longer poem. I suspect that not all who sing it are aware that in the proper context "the heat of our desire" refers to unbridled lust!

3   The many references to such phenomena in the Psalms are taken by Old Testament scholars to reflect the general pattern of Israel's worship. They should therefore be seen as quite normal.

2   A PERSONAL JOURNEY

Born a "peace child" at the end of the Second World War, nurtured in the arms of the people-sensitive Free Church tradition, at the age of thirteen I was also a child of the age. I had imbibed a sense that humankind (including myself) was in control of its destiny, and that this destiny included a successful career in the sciences, which held the key to constant progress.

But not all was quite so well. Outside, there was the growing cloud of nuclear destruction and the darkening red threat from the inexorable onward march of Communism. Inside there was also an awareness (mainly dismissed) that I was alone in a vast universe and somehow incomplete. One evening spent listening to the stories of teenage friends who had discovered the difference that a living relationship with Jesus Christ makes, proved to be a key experience. Twice that night I sensed God was speaking directly to me, and twice, by myself, by my response, a steel door closed between us. The first response implied God needed people like me to help him get the Church out of the mess it was in. The second, that I would agree to meet up with Jesus, because it was the obvious thing to do; I would join the club for nice people.

By the end of that evening I was inwardly desolate. I knew that God had given me not just one chance, but two. I understood very clearly that pride and peer pressure were not acceptable to God. I had thrown his loving offer back in his face. The night was dark and damp, typical for November. Inside me it seemed as though, like a rocket meant to go into orbit round a planet, I had missed its gravitational pull and I was now heading for the endless dark emptiness of outer space.

I walked home, as I often did, with our youth leader, Eric. Half-way there, I prayed a silent yet definite and desperate prayer: "God, if you are there, get Eric to ask me if I'm a Christian. He'll be able to help me!" Three steps later he put the question and my journey had truly begun. Did I ask or did God prompt?

That sense of God's presence never quite left me even when theologians announced conclusively "God's dead". Perhaps the next stage, however, was fifteen years later, when a few people from the Baptist Church where I was now minister, started breathing a new air, and singing new songs. There too, in a small group, the longing for Christ's healing ministry today was rekindled for us. That group was my first real experience of the creative power of a small group, committed to one another with acceptance and love, but also pursuing God and the things of the Kingdom.

Just prior to this group's formation I had stumbled on a new way of approaching the Bible. A woman was seeking direction for her life, and none of the pastoral approaches I had tried before seemed pertinent. Somehow, and I don't really know how or why it happened, I started to introduce her to journeying into the Scriptures, using her imagination, in the security of passages which held some of the dynamics of her situation. Of course, in order to prepare myself for these sessions, I had to explore this approach myself. I too found that Scripture, as well as what I sensed to be Christ's presence and direction, were experienced in a more immediate way. I felt there was something wholesome and integrating about this approach.

Although it was in some way new, I realized it had antecedents in good preaching which also invited people to enter imaginatively into Scripture. A passage from one of Leslie Weatherhead's books[1] illustrates clearly what I mean. I still recall the deep gratitude and relief which came to me when I first read it. This was at a time when, as a newish Christian, I was being unsettled by doubts and self-questioning. It spoke to me at a very deep level.

> *Let me close with one other imaginative picture which has meant much to me since I first read it. I think it is to be ascribed to the genius of Dr H R L Sheppard, though I have taken the liberty of altering and enlarging it. Its purpose is to bring you that sense of the presence of Jesus which the writer regards as central to the experience of the Christian.*
>
> > *It is evening. The Sea of Galilee lies before your eyes. In the west the splendid scarlets and golds have faded. It is the moment of daffodil and pale green sky. To your left, mountains run down steeply to the sea. Jesus is climbing up a spur of one of these mountains, seeking quietude in the bosom of the hills and in the hush of night; seeking to push back the tumultuous demands of all there is to do, to make a silence in which the soul can breathe, to pray. You can see his figure outlined for a moment against the*

fading light of that last glow of evening. But, in the east, clouds have gathered; clouds that mean storm. Rank upon rank, battalion upon battalion, they sweep westward. The water of the lake turns from amber to steel. The wind that went to summon the storm returns in front of it, majestically, heralding its advent. It strikes chill and cold, menacing, almost. Then the swish of rain. Jesus hears it long before it reaches Him. He seeks in front of Him a shepherd's hut on the hillside. He makes for it to avoid the discomfort of a soaking, lights the simple lamp He finds within, and kneels to pray.

Now imagine that you are on the mountain too. The storm is on you. You see a light shining from the window of the hut. Panting and dishevelled, you rush up to it, seeking shelter. Glancing through the window, you see who is there, and you turn away. Shelter or no shelter, you feel you cannot intrude on his seclusion. But he has heard you. He rises, flings open the door. For you there is his smile, his word of welcome. Then the door closes. Just you and Jesus. Jesus and you.

I found opportunities coming my way to share this approach in group contexts and began to realize that people were owning God's truth in a deeper and more personal way.[2] I gradually began to realize that there was no guarantee the Scriptures were meant to be understood with the kind of analytical approach that years of grammar school and university theological education had given me. Maybe this kind of imaginative encounter was as legitimate as the one in which I had been schooled. Such thoughts were clarified and strengthened by Walter Schlink's book.[3]

Meanwhile I had moved to Coventry. That move itself had involved me in another very powerful experience of God. He had spoken to me with amazing directness about it months before it happened. It also included a near-miss accident which helped to convince me that I really did believe in God and heaven (I had been taught to question how I can know anything for certain – Descartes almost ruled supreme!). Other books began to add to the growing sense that God does communicate with us in deeply personal ways. Two authors in particular proved to be productive allies. John Powell's delicate and beautiful story caused resonance and amplification for me. Here is a moment of significance.

> *It happened on a definite Friday evening in the early Spring...*
> *With all the suddenness and jolt of a heart attack, I was filled*
> *with an experiential awareness of the presence of God within*
> *me. It has been said that no one can convey an experience*
> *to another, but can offer only his reflections on that*
> *experience... I can only say, in trying to share my experience*
> *with you, that I felt like a balloon being blown up with the*
> *pure pleasure of God's loving presence, even to the point of*
> *discomfort and doubt that I could hold any more of this*
> *sudden ecstasy. I think of the song "He touched Me!", sung by*
> *Barbra Streisand, as the most apt way to describe the*
> *experience of that night... I remember thinking that the touch*
> *of God excited a whole new vision and perception of life. It*
> *was like putting on badly needed glasses for the first time. A*
> *whole new and very beautiful world comes into view, and this*
> *new way of seeing things somehow diminishes the importance*
> *of every previous vision... It was more than I could have*
> *dreamed in all my technicolour dreams.* [4]

John Powell is honest enough to admit that this experience was not
enough to last his lifetime. There was to be a quite lengthy period
of decline in the quality of his awareness of God, brought on, he
suspects, by his very strong competitive drive. Then through the
gentle approach of a neurotic woman he had been counselling for
some time who was dramatically changed through meeting with
Jesus, John began to change too.

> *What began to happen in me almost immediately can be*
> *compared only to Springtime. It seemed as though I had*
> *been through a long, hard-frozen wintertime. My heart and*
> *soul had suffered all the bareness, the nakedness of nature*
> *in winter. Now, in this Springtime of the spirit, it seemed as*
> *though the veins of my soul were thawing, as though blood*
> *was beginning to course through my soul again.*

> *Once more I had the sensation of putting on a new pair of*
> *badly needed glasses and seeing all kinds of things that had*
> *been obscured.* [5]

With so much of this I could identify, and I still can.

In Joyce Hugget too, I sensed a person who was travelling a
road, similar to mine, but who was many miles ahead, both in her
experiences, and in her power to communicate it clearly and
helpfully to others. Her book, which first caught my attention, was

Listening to God.[6] In the second chapter she describes her visit to Mount St Bernard's Abbey, a place I knew well, because it was only a few miles from my first pastorate. This gave her experience an added significance for me, because, geographically speaking, our journeys had intersected! Listen to what she says.

> *I shall never forget that first sip of real stillness. The retreat demanded nothing of us except simply to be in the presence of God. Coming, as we had, straight from the activism of parish life in a busy city-centre church, this absence of the driving need to achieve was therapy in itself. The monastery, with its prayer-saturated walls and fabric, its quiet rhythm and its God-centredness, seemed to us a welcome oasis. We were being nourished, renewed and refreshed. We each rejoiced to watch each other relax in the warmth of the felt love of Christ, a phenomenon which seemed rare at home.*[7]

Later on she describes another visit to the same abbey. What is important to note is how she senses an openness of all her being before God:

> *What I heard in those times of listening was more than a voice. It was a presence. Yes. I heard the Lord call my name. But I also "heard" his tenderness. I soaked up his love. And this listening was on a level which runs deeper than mere words. Sometimes it seems as though Jesus himself stood in front of me or above me. This encounter with him overwhelmed me. Was it his radiance? Was it the tenderness of his gaze? Or was it the fact of his gaze? The only way I can describe it is to liken it to the overwhelming a person feels when they love someone very deeply. That person's heart burns with pure pleasure at the joy of being in the presence of the loved one, that person's eyes sparkle or shine or mist over with warmth or deep felt emotion, but that person does not speak. No words are necessary. They might even be intrusive for they could trivialise the love. And nothing must spoil the ecstasy of their encounter which may be all too brief in any case. They are content simply "to be" in one another's presence. But that silence is packed with warm communication.*

> *I had never delighted in God in this way before. And it had never occurred to me that God wanted me to linger in his presence so that he could show me that he delighted in me.*[8]

Joyce Hugget confirmed the legitimacy of many of the things I was experiencing out of the riches of God's grace. Her book gave me confidence and encouragement to continue. I found her confirmation of the kind of approach to the Bible I had "discovered" positive too.[9]

But for Joyce it is essentially the romantic, the religious, and the rural which are powerful triggers.

> *In this place [Mount St Bernard's] he touches me, the real me which often I hide from the world. He touches me through the wideness of the music, he touches me through the visual stimulus of the cross, he touches me through the powerful, prayerful atmosphere, he touches me through the flickering candle which somehow stills my harassed heart.[10]*

Another meditation Joyce remembers clearly was one led by Stephen Verney.

> *I recall the Saturday well. The sun shone on the Derbyshire hills which encircled the bishop's house. The hedgerows and meadows were studded with wild flowers: harebells, buttercups, meadow's-sweet, cowslips. We stood on the terrace of the bishop's home, drank coffee, and drank in, too, that magnificence of the countryside in summer. Then we went inside.*

> *As we sat in a circle in the lounge, the bishop invited us to focus our attention on a bowl of wild flowers on a small table in the centre of the circle. "Just waste time looking at them," he invited. After a few minutes he turned to Matthew 6 and read Jesus' command: "Consider the lilies..." "This word 'consider' really means 'contemplate'", the bishop suggested. "When we contemplate something, we look at it from many angles, we touch it, feel it, smell it and learn from it. That is what I propose we do this morning."*

> *He passed the bowl of flowers round the room and invited each person to choose one.[11]*

I am very grateful to Joyce. As she herself wrote,

> *God has wonderful ways of bringing people, events and books into our lives just when we need them.[12]*

She was such an author for me. But something even then was uneasy with the focus of her meditations. It took several years for me to become conscious enough of that unease to verbalize it. For me, however, the issue was becoming, "Is God not present in our busy, modern world, too?"

Meanwhile a new element was beginning to reach me. I began to hear of John Wimber, of "Signs and Wonders", of "Power Evangelism" with the renewed emphasis on the miraculous and the associated growth of the healing ministries within many churches. Partly because I was not a great conference goer and partly because of other commitments, it was to be a long while before I actually got to a Wimber conference. Perhaps this was a good thing, for in many ways it meant I forged my own approach, and in some ways it made me more directly aware of God. Nevertheless, the visit of one of the Vineyard teams to Coventry proved a watershed in my life. I only attended one of the four sessions, even though our church building was the venue. When the Vineyard leader invited church leaders to go forward for prayer I went forward with a naïve openness for God to do whatever he wanted and a confidence that I was a strong male and would not end up on the floor! The most important element was an unquenchable longing to be God's person, through and through. The details of that night are not relevant. What exactly happened to me I shall never appreciate, but it certainly took me one more step (at least) in openness to God.

It so happened that within a few days I was leading an imaginative Bible study with a group that had been considering different approaches to Bible study. In the quiet reflective part,[13] one person began to sob and groan. That person was unaware of the kind of thing that might be expected to happen at a "Wimber meeting", but rather than dampening the emotional depths that were surfacing through encounter with Scripture, we were now (somewhat) ready to accept and minister to the person as they were. The effect on the group was very surprising, as several of the people, most of whom knew little if anything about Wimber, were profoundly affected. This was an important experience for me, in that it brought together several aspects of my journey and convinced me that behind John Wimber's ministry was the effective involvement of the Holy Spirit and not merely clever techniques of group dynamics.

Gradually, I learnt that God really did reveal things to his people today, things that were not necessarily supernatural in themselves, but the knowing of which was difficult to account for without supernatural explanations. I learnt that God gave such "revelations" not to condemn and manipulate people but to bring healing and release. I learnt that often he gave one part of the picture to one person and another to a different person, so that corporate confidence was an important ingredient and helped to explain why such awareness had been suppressed in other contexts. I also realized that God often, but by no means always, used objects or images from our immediate physical or personal environment as triggers for the messages he gives. These understandings came partly through the development of a group within our church which prayed with people for healing, and partly through a course I led jointly with another person, called "Open to God". It was also on this course I began to realize that much "modern meditation" was locked into the rural and the romantic rather than our real world, whereas God, at least in my experience, used very mundane and contemporary objects to help communicate.

Two other "encounters" focused this dawning awareness. As part of a day of training with our church leadership we went, after lunch, on an Emmaus walk. This was another new experience to which I was introduced. Most of my meditative and imaginative experiences had been static ones. The idea was that we went in pairs, for a gentle walk in different directions from the country chapel where we were spending the day. It was a cool, grey February day and I walked our circuit with a rather quiet and reserved deacon. Making conversation was easier than I had anticipated, but the pressure to maintain a conversation I found something of a distraction from hearing God. Certainly, after we had walked a good half of our journey, I was not very hopeful of returning with anything very significant, but then it didn't matter anyway. Being February, the hedgerows were bare. As we walked I noticed all kinds of litter thrown or caught in them – plastic in various forms was the worst culprit, from scraps of polythene bags to large white plastic containers, but there were many other things too; a pile of cigarette stubs where obviously a car had stopped and the ash tray had been emptied, for instance. Almost unawares, I was beginning to sense a growing anger that this countryside had been spoilt by the thoughtless discarding of litter by countless people. As we were about to turn to take the road back into the village, my anger became focused. Someone had dumped a whole collection of now rusting tin cans. What was more, there was tangled bailing string too. Because this spread of pollution focused my anger, my eyes stopped with it for longer than the other scraps that we had passed. How could anyone be so callous, I was thinking? Then the truth dawned! This was no ordinary rubbish;

these cans tied together with string had previously been attached to a car bumper. They represented a gift of friendship and celebration. On someone's wedding day, "friends" had garlanded the car to add a note of excitement to the honeymoon couple's departure. Here, as soon as it was safe, they had stopped to remove the embarrassing but welcome tangle. Rusting tins and tangled string were, properly understood, the sign of love and laughter, celebration, family, and friends. Strangely, they had carried a message of far greater importance and far greater significance than the rubbish they "really" were. I soon realized that God was speaking to me about groups of people, about collections of experience in people's lives, about other everyday, throwaway objects, like bread, or a bowl and towel, that he could use to show people a celebration of his love and care. The message was very different to the objects; here was a profound parable of what God could do with any object or experience from our world. He could amaze us by speaking his truth to us through it, in spite of its apparent nature.

This experience has always remained a vivid and living one. It is not surprising, then, that when I was asked to lead a day for another church's leadership team, I should include an after lunch Emmaus walk. This time I definitely did not expect very much for me. But God is a God of surprises. After the confined space and intensity of interacting with the group for two-and-a-half hours I was ready to escape. While they set off in pairs, I meandered back to my car to pick up a few requirements for the next session. My car was parked in the pub car park next to the church. It was a large, open air car park surrounded by a newish fence, beyond which was a field scattered with thistle stalks and a few sheep. I sensed myself being drawn towards the fence and began to suspect God might be wanting to say something to me, but, of course, without any certainty. Probably it will be through the sheep, I thought. When I reached the fence, I leant on it, and wondered. I gazed at the sheep but nothing much came to mind. Then, as though from a voice, I heard, "Look down". Beyond my reach, unless I climbed the fence, was an empty beer glass, partially hidden in the withered scrub which bordered the field. Someone, perhaps on a hot summer's day, had quenched their thirst, resting on the fence as I had done, then, instead of taking the glass back to the bar, they had thrown it down. What a waste. I wanted to gather up the glass and "take it back home", where it could be washed and used, filled and fulfilled again. The emotion was strangely powerful for a beer glass. I didn't pick it up – the pub was closed – and so I left it there, feeling slightly guilty.

Then I turned away and walked alone down the lane towards the village. There were some impressive country cottages, one in particular transformed from an old mill. I was still gazing at this "des res" when a voice said, "Now, look down". As I did, looking towards the bottom of the hawthorn hedge, I saw another discarded beer glass. I felt the same strange longing to pick it up and return it to the place where it would be valued, cleaned, and fulfilled. It seemed such a waste, carelessly disposed of, potentially dangerous if it broke, but whole and ready to be reclaimed. I realized that God was speaking to me about the many people who, for whatever reason, have found themselves detached from the Church, away from their home. If I could feel so strongly for an empty beer glass, no wonder a shepherd could for his lost sheep, a woman for her marriage coin, and God for his lost people.

Such experiences told me that God could speak to us through the standard objects of our contemporary world. They were clear and powerful moments on a journey I was already taking. They were rocket booster moments, giving fresh momentum, but also moments where the direction I was travelling received significant readjustment.

Gradually, I began to pay more attention to the ordinary world around me. The more I thought about it the more sense it made that God could communicate through the world around me. If we could express profound and important truths through a sequence of squiggles on a page, why should God not use a sequence of objects or events. If a mother can express her love to her baby through squeezing it and changing nappies, why shouldn't God, through the impact of our world on us, and the sordid side of our environment too. But for me, an important check on my experiences and my speculations was what Scripture had to say about all this. Unless there was scriptural warrant for what I was discovering I had better beware.

Suggested Activities

1. Note any of the author's experiences or reflections which you find especially significant. Why did these strike you as important? Is it because they challenge your position, or because they confirm and strengthen inclinings you have?

2. Recall any books, especially Christian ones, which you sense have made a significant contribution to your growth as a Christian. Reflect on the times in your life when you read them, and then seek to understand why they were important to you; does this indicate how God teaches you?

3. Consider any experiences akin to meditation that you have had and still value. If you have friends who are reading this book too, or if you sense others are also involved in Christian meditation, try and begin to share your experiences, and encourage others to let you into their special times.

Notes

1 L. D. Weatherhead *Jesus & Ourselves*, first published 1930; this edition 1957, pp. 126–8.

2 A more detailed explanation, together with an opportunity to try this approach, will be found on pp. 61–76.

3 *Transforming Bible Study* (London, 1981).

4 John Powell SJ, *He Touched Me: my pilgrimage of Prayer* (Allert. Texas, 1974), pp. 16–22.

5 Op. cit., pp. 53–4.

6 Joyce Hugget *Listening to God* (Hodder & Stoughton, London, 1986), p. 25.

7 Op. cit., p. 25.

8 Op. cit., pp. 33–4.

9 Op. cit., pp. 154–7.

10 Op. cit., p. 33.

11 Op. cit., p. 120.

12 Op. cit., p. 41.

13 For details of this process, see Chapter 6.

3 THE BIBLICAL BASIS

In Chapter 2 I shared with you some of the significant "moments" in my life. These were significant in that they helped me move towards exploring meditation as a Christian means of meeting with God and learning from him. I also hoped that by sharing something of myself, other people would understand more clearly why I want us to be willing to see our contemporary secular modern world as a focus for such meditations.

In this chapter I want to look at the scriptural basis for such a view. If you like, Chapter 2 gives the subjective, personal, reason why I am committed to this kind of approach and Chapter 3 gives the objective foundations for it.

Joyce Huggett has already made an excellent contribution in her book *Listening to God* (see especially Chapters 7–12). There she explains how, as she searched through Scripture, she discovered the biblical warrant for her kind of meditation. I would encourage those who wish to establish the propriety of Christian meditation in general terms to consult her writings. I am sure I would find it difficult to improve on her considerations. Rather, I want to see if Scripture also encourages and endorses my experience that God can be found through our world, with its industry and sometimes manufactured ugliness. As the most recent Scriptures were written almost 2,000 years ago, we cannot expect them to deal with the details of our technological environment. But if we are prepared to look beneath the surface issues Scripture may, and in my opinion does, help us considerably. Our concern can be expressed in the following question. Does Scripture show that God speaks to and meets with people through the work place and the rubbish heap, or only in the beautiful places of creation? Equally important is the way Scripture expresses God's relationship with the world and the role of people in it; do these factors support the view that God can reveal himself in the work place? The whole of this book could be devoted to these points, but I content myself with a few indications. I have, therefore, created a collage of insights so that the "pictures" come from different kinds of biblical material, and are reflected through different levels of scholarly approach. Each picture indicates a much larger resource that could be utilized if we were wanting to construct a comprehensive picture. But why do we need scriptural support anyway? If it works, isn't that enough?

For those who are committed to Christian meditation it can never be sufficient to claim "it works". We also need to provide proper scriptural validation.

For me, Scripture has final authority in every aspect of my spiritual path. It directs me to the end of it all. It is God who is "alpha and omega, the beginning and the end", to him belong all praise and glory. Hence, my own spiritual enjoyment or achievement can never take precedent over the end to which I must tend. The only justification for my spiritual development is that in some way "his glory", from which through sin I have fallen, is being restored. So, Scripture makes clear the end or purpose for my journey, however, Scripture is crucial too in determining the means to this.

All Scripture is inspired by God and is useful for teaching the truth, rebuking error, correcting faults and giving instruction.

2 Timothy 3.16

I accept wholeheartedly that:

The Scripture says, Man cannot live on bread alone, but needs every word that God speaks.

Matthew 4.4

So we need the Scriptures to guide and correct us in our thinking and our doing. Without the constant replenishing of our total selves with the reality of God, individually and collectively human beings diminish in their humanity. But part of the truth of Scripture is that "every word God speaks" is not restricted to the words that are written. It is Scripture itself which affirms that God's will and ways and wonder are writ large in the sky.

How clearly the sky reveals God's glory, how plainly it shows what he has done.

Psalm 19.1

Further, his imprimatur is stamped on the earth:

You set the mountains in place by your strength,
Showing your mighty power.
You calm the roar of the seas and the noise of the waves;
You calm the uproar of the peoples.

*The whole world stands in awe of the great
things that you have done.
Your deeds bring shouts of joy from one end
of the earth to another.*

Psalm 65.6–8

But his kindness as well as his power, his real character as well as his naked authority, are etched into our world, as the Psalms indicate.

*You show your care for the land by sending rain;
You make it rich and fertile.*

Psalm 65.9

God's goodness to his people is displayed in the fruitfulness of harvest.

The land has produced its harvest, God our God has blessed it.

Psalm 67.6

The desired consequence is "that the world may know your will; so that all nations may know your salvation" (Psalm 67.2 – compare 67.7).

Such outbursts of awareness and desire are like the outcrop of rock through the grass on a hillside. They reveal what is everywhere present but hidden; what gives shape to the whole scene; what affects the growth of the grass and trees by providing fixture for the roots and drainage for the soil. For the basis of such openness to God in the midst of the world is that the same God whose reality is revealed in Scripture has spoken into the world's creation.

The context in which all human life is lived and in which all Scripture is written is Genesis chapter 1, where, like the key theme of a magnificent symphony we hear:

Then God commanded... it was done... And God was pleased with what he saw.

As Paul puts it within the New Testament context:

Ever since God created the world, his invisible qualities, both his eternal power and his divine nature have been clearly seen.

Romans 1.20

This is scriptural truth and an important theological grounding for all valid Christian approaches to meditation. Scripture recognizes that God's reality can be recognized and experienced within creation. If this were not so, if all the world were not at least opaque to his reality, we would be creating idols in our own image, admiring our own reflection in the mirror, instead of meeting with the living God.

However, Scripture is also careful not to deify nature. Indeed, in large measure Scripture is a story of the disasters which happen when the human race worships the created rather than the creator. So, we constantly need to check our present awareness of God's reality and immediacy with the bench marker of his personality and truth as given to us in Scripture.

But if God's truth is there in Scripture, why bother with seeking him in and through the world? Why spend time gazing into a candle or spending time alone on Lindisfarne for days?

There are many reasons but here are a few which seem to be significant.

1. There is something special and immediate about meeting God through some kind of focused meditation or even "chance" revelation. It is not dissimilar to the heart-quenching excitement which happens when we go to church and the minister seems to be preaching to "no one but me", because the message seems direct, straight into our personal situation. We sense God's special care for us, it releases in us new strength to go on with and for God. The same can happen with our daily Bible reading too. This for me does not render the openness to God in our daily lives unnecessary; rather it confirms both the validity of the experience of our encounter with God (both "types" of revelation have a similar resonance for us) and encourages us to look for it there in the world. In the end, whether it is through a sermon, or considering Scripture, or through meditative reflection is secondary. It is what God chooses to show us of himself, to do for us, and enable us to become that matters. My own observation is that often through "the world based encounter" he reaches more deeply into people with life-changing power. But I gladly acknowledge his sovereignty in all of this; God chooses whichever mode he wills, and it may vary from person to person and from time to time.

2. It helps to develop a healthy excitement and anticipation for every day and each part of the day. If God can meet us through his world and ours, then who knows what the day can bring.

3. Finding that God may show us something of himself through our everyday world leads on to a care for the world and every human experience. Because God can be in our environment for us, nothing is purely secular. Such an experience does for us, as Christian people, what modern poetry or modern sculpture can do for us as contemporary people. Sometimes a modern sculptor can take a collection of rubbish or a pile of rubble and create a new image which has power. When this happens the sculpture communicates understanding and some "light" within us reverberates in response. This is achieved by the interplay of an artistic imagination, with a sensitivity to the realities which the rubble represents in our society, fused by ability and sheer hard work. The consequence may well be that we look at the rubbish in our society in new ways. We can no longer disregard it for we have been shown its potential. So when we start to find God speaking to us in our world we begin to value it differently. Again this change of attitude has many counterparts in other dimensions of our human experience.

So far we have established that Scripture teaches us that because God has created the world, he can reveal himself through it, and therefore we can find him in the created world. This is our endorsement, in general terms, for seeking and expecting encounters with God as we spend time face to face with his creation – whether on a large scale by gazing at the stars or the micro scale by looking into the heart of a flower. So those who help us to learn the art of meditation are helping to increase our openness to God. It is somewhat like the discovery of "body language"; until then we may have thought we were only being addressed by people's spoken words. Once we understand about "body language" we begin to realize that all along we were being given and receiving another level of message. With our increased awareness we pick up a lot more from now on and we do it at a more conscious level.

What we have not yet done is established that through and in the world and works of "human beings" we can expect to meet with God. It is one thing to anticipate that God can speak to us through the glory of a sunset over the lakes and another through the noise of a sawmill. It is the latter that I am after!

But this is where we need to bring in an even more important insight from Scripture. Through "the Word" God made all things; not one thing in all creation was made without him (John 1.3).

This is another way of saying that all creation is by God's word, and that therefore it bears his stamp on it. But the New Testament goes on to say; "The Word became a human being and, full of grace and truth, lived among us" (John 1.14).

Clearly, this is the very centre of the Christian position – it is in Jesus that God is most vividly and readily to be found. He is the ultimate revelation. But not only revelation, he is the source of redemption too. For we need to be able to perceive God, and without the divine operation of redemption we are blind to the light of God's truth. However, this is not the only direction in which this dynamic verse of Christian truth takes us.

What it also does is show us that human life, in all its aspects, interactions, and activities has the potential for revealing God. This focal point of clarity in John's Gospel is not alone by any means; it flows back to the Old Testament insight that God made people in his own image;[1] it picks up on the theme of man being or bearing the glory of God which he has disfigured but not destroyed (Romans 3.23). It links into the Christian reality that we are being transformed into Christ's likeness, that is being changed from one degree of glory to another and so "reflect the glory of the Lord" (2 Corinthians 3.18).

Taken together these insights push us towards an expectation that within our human lives, our relationships, our creative actions, even within our failures and sin, individually and corporately, there is the potential for us to find truth about God and so meet with him.

The justification for "meditation" is to be founded on God as creator; this frees us to experience God in the world he has made. However, the justification is not to be restricted to creation; it should also include Christology, that is our understanding of who Jesus is, and what this implies for human being and doing. This opens up many gateways into human experience as the locus for our meetings with God.

So, I am convinced that such biblical considerations do establish the validity of the process that is the basis for this book. However, the Bible helps us in another way, that is by illustrating the point I am making. So, while we do not have the space to conduct a complete survey of the evidence, any more than we had room for a complete theology of meditation, it is worth while presenting a sample of the kinds of material I have in mind.

Behind much biblical material there is a background awareness of God in the world that was contemporary to the human authors. The prophets of the Old Testament are a good place to start. It has become a common place for understanding the faith of the Old Testament to say that "God acts in history" – this itself has fascinating implications for our approach. However, it is not only in the unfolding of political events and historical memories that the prophets met with God. Amos is the earliest prophet whose sayings have been collected together into a "book". His "writings" represent a significant watershed for Israel's understanding of God. It is to his encounters with God that we turn first.

In Amos 4.13 we find the following words:

> *God is the one who made the mountains*
> *and created the winds.*
> *He makes his thoughts known to people;*
> *he changes day into night.*
> *He walks on the heights of the earth.*
> *This is his name: the Lord God Almighty!*

This verse affirms belief in the creative work of God and in his revelation to humankind; both foundational beliefs for those who want to find God through meditation, understood as an openness for God to speak to us and meet us in and through the natural world and our perception of it. Moreover, in saying "This is his name: the Lord God Almighty", there is implied the view that through our perception of creation we can experience the reality of the God of Israel. For this is what "name" means – the character, the reality of the one named.

This general standpoint is made specific through some of Amos's visions. Chapter 7 gives us ample illustrations. In his visions Amos sees a number of natural phenomena, part of the created world such as a swarm of locusts, fire, and a basket of fruit, and God speaks through them to him about Israel's predicament and God's attitude to Israel. Furthermore, Amos enters into an intercessory relationship with God because of his visions. While it is true they are described as "visions" rather than the result of meditation on natural phenomena, the material on which they are based is indicative of the power of the created world to be a vehicle of revelation. If you wish, we can say they are one stage removed from meditative awareness, but they establish its potential.

However, it is not only the "natural world" that is involved. The world of people is also intertwined. It is there in the vision of the locusts; for part of the impact of the vision is that the locusts start to attack the young shoots, which are growing "after the King's share of the grass had been cut". Here is the world of work and of political structure becoming an inherent component of the revelation.

This is even more the case in the famous vision about the plumb line.

> *I had another vision from the Lord. In it I saw him standing beside a wall that had been built with the help of a plumb line, and there was a plumb line in his hand. He asked me, "Amos, what do you see?"*
>
> *"A plumb line," I answered.*
>
> *Then he said, "I am using it to show that my people are like a wall that is out of line. I will not change my mind again about punishing them. The places where Isaac's descendants worship will be destroyed. The holy places of Israel will be left in ruins. I will bring the dynasty of King Jeroboam to an end."*

Amos 7.7–9

Here very clearly it is the world of work and ancient technology which provide the components for this vision.

We can see other components in the process of meditation in the words of God's judgement on Israel, as expressed by Amos. There are many references to the "goings on" of his day – things he has clearly observed and through which God's word has come – people being sold into slavery because they cannot pay their debts, clothing taken from the poor as security for loans, the perversion of justice through bribery, the corruption in commerce through the fixing of the weights. Amos meets God's mind through these observations. Two points are especially pertinent. The first is that this is a "negative encounter" – but it still makes God's revelation through the law a more pertinent and immediate experience – which is one of the tonal contributions of meditation. Secondly, it is not the observation of human activity alone which leads to revelation; it is clearly in the light of God's revelation through the law of Israel that these observed phenomena spring to life. I suspect it normally is the case, that the observed phenomena need at least some residual revelation in order to gain their power of immediacy and encounter with God. Without a substructure of biblical revelation today's phenomena may well remain silent.

Amos is interesting for our purposes in another respect. Frequently he speaks in what sounds remarkably like proverbs.

*Do two people start travelling together without arranging to
    meet?*
Does a lion roar in the forest unless he has found a victim?
*Does a young lion growl in his den unless he has caught
    something?*
Does a bird get caught in a trap if the trap has not been baited?
Does a trap spring unless something sets it off?
*Does the war trumpet sound in a city without making the people
    afraid?*
Does disaster strike a city unless the Lord sends it?
*The Sovereign Lord never does anything without revealing his
    plan to his servants, the prophets.*
When a lion roars, who can avoid being afraid?

                                                    Amos 3.3–8

Proverbs are like fossilized meditations, compressed perhaps by the pressures of repetition; fixed by the rhythms of speech, but containing concentrated observations of the world. Yet, without some relationship to their real world, they lose their power.

If proverbs are understood as "fossilized meditations" they help us understand the waves of continuity between human observation – wisdom – divine wisdom and God's creative power which are traceable in the Books of Proverbs and Job.

*Wisdom can make your life pleasant and lead you safely
through it. Those who become wise are happy, wisdom will
give them life. The Lord created the earth by his wisdom;
by his knowledge he set the sky in place.*

                                              Proverbs 3.16, 18–19

The way Amos uses proverbial sayings endorses the sense that "meditation" is an important pathway for prophetic revelation. Amos then introduces us to a variety of ways in which the observation of the world around him leads to an understanding of who God is. Jeremiah, another prophet, confirms this but also moves us forward, for in his case there are illustrations of even greater immediacy.

Following the brief but illuminating account of Jeremiah's call to be a prophet, we are presented with his two opening "visions"; the first of the almond tree and the second of the boiling pot in the north (Jeremiah 1.1–19). Whether either or both of these should be correlated with immediate observations which become the vehicle for revelation is not absolutely clear. The almond branch is often understood this way but it could have been as "visionary" as the boiling pot. Equally Jeremiah could have been observing both "out in the real world".[2] What is undoubtedly clear is that observation did lead on to revelation for Jeremiah, for sometimes he tells us it did.

Probably the instance which comes most readily to mind is his visit to the "potter's house".

So I went there and saw the potter working at his wheel. Whenever a piece of pottery turned out imperfect, he would take the clay and make it something else.

Jeremiah 18.3–4

Here is Jeremiah observing not unspoilt creation, not the natural tranquil world, not even someone lovingly involved with their creative hobby and relaxation. Rather, we have Jeremiah spiritually immersed in his world of technology and industry. It is, moreover, not the positive, successful outcome which reveals God's attitude, but the negative.

Whenever a piece of pottery turned out imperfect he would take the clay and make it something else.

Jeremiah 18.4

Jeremiah becomes aware of God's perspectives not only by what he observes but also by the potter's manufacturing processes.

The well-known incident of the conflict with the prophet Hananiah also revolves around such an experience, Jeremiah makes himself "A yoke out of leather straps and wooden crossbars" (Jeremiah 27.2) and he wears it on his neck. This leads to a dramatic conflict with the prophet Hananiah with further revelation from God (Jeremiah 28.10–17) leading ultimately to Hananiah's death. Revelation involves the processes of manufacturing agricultural "machinery".

The prophets also suggest that the religious environment may also contribute to our meetings with God. The story of Isaiah's call in Chapter 6 suggests this.

In the year that King Uzziah died, I saw the Lord. He was sitting on his throne, high and exalted, and his robe filled the whole Temple. Round him flaming creatures were standing, each of which had six wings. Each creature covered its face with two wings, and its body with two, and used the other two for flying. They were calling out to each

other: "Holy, holy, holy! The Lord Almighty is holy! His
glory fills the world." The sound of their voices made the
foundations of the Temple shake, and the Temple itself was
filled with smoke.

Isaiah 6.1–4

It is not clear at all whether the whole account is based simply on a vision or whether the vision is based on some occasion when Isaiah was in the temple and the normal temple worship was transposed into another realm. My own reading of the situation is the latter. In any case, whether directly or indirectly, the observable reality of the temple, the building, its artefacts, and its rituals, contribute to Isaiah's earth-shaking and prophet-shaping experience with God. This encourages us to expect that not only in the "world of work", but also in the "world of worship" there is potential for experiencing something fresh from God. So, towards the end of our book, when we have sought to develop our appetite and aptitude for becoming aware of God in "the real world" we will seek to bend back our enhanced receptivity into the context of our worship.

Before we leave the Old Testament and step into the New, for more and varied illustrations, I want to make one fundamental point. I do not intend to imply that we are like grape treaders who only have to tramp around and inevitably we shall be rewarded with an oozing of divine revelation at our feet. It is important to recognize God's sovereignty in all these experiences. Of course, it is true that if God has created the world then somehow it points to him who made it, as a picture does the artist, or a play the dramatist. Equally, if people are made in God's image, even though that image is blurred and twisted by sin, there is still some correlation between the image and God which we can discern. However, what we are looking for through Christian meditation goes beyond this, although it may include the perception of God in this way. What satisfies us in seeking for God by openness to his world are those times when God bursts through the continuum, concentrates its potential for his contact with us, and he chooses to reveal himself. This implies his free choice in the process. The prophets suggest one way in which this works. They often indicate that they see what they do, because they are following out divine instructions. If they were disobedient they would not be in the right place to "hear" God through their world. For us too, as illustrated in the second of my personal stories (Chapter 2, p. 19), there will often be a sense of divine preparation or guidance in the selection of where we go, what we do, or on what we focus.

The converse of this is that we must be willing for God to choose not to meet with us. Bill Hybels in his stimulating book *Too Busy not to Pray*, has this to say:

> *Sometimes when I wait quietly for God to speak, I sense total silence from heaven. It's as if no one is at home. I have felt very silly in these times. Did I ask the wrong questions? Was I foolish to expect answers? Was God really listening?*
>
> *After thinking about it, I don't need to feel upset if God sometimes chooses to remain silent. He's a living being, and he speaks when he has something to say.*

What Bill Hybels applies to our relationship with God in prayer also applies to our experience of God through reflecting on his world. We shall also find his perceptivity helpful when we think about why, if at all, we should cultivate our ability to "touch base with God" in our everyday experiences. All I want to establish at this point is that we are not talking about having "God on demand"; we cannot crush the vintage out by our own efforts. Yet we should remember there is no hope of wine without the right raw materials!

The Old Testament then has yielded helpful illustrations of people being impacted by God's reality as they look at the world around them, both the created world and the market place of people.

What of the New Testament?

One of the most significant features to be considered is that of the parables of Jesus. They are full of incidental references to the everyday world in which he lived. T.R. Glover was a scholar of a previous generation who was fascinated by this fact. He presented his observations in an unusual way, in a children's hymn, relating life for Jesus in the workshop of Joseph and the home of Mary. Here are three of the many stanzas:

> *Where is the coin that fell? With her broom*
> *Mary goes sweeping over the room,*
> *In the home at Nazareth.*
>
> *Look, there it is! She ran in her joy*
> *Telling the news to the man and the boy,*
> *In the shop at Nazareth.*
>
> *Patching their clothes by the candlelight,*
> *Mary would sew far into the night,*
> *In the home at Nazareth.* [3]

The point T.R. Glover was making is that the parables did not just appear from nowhere. Although they were and continue to be a powerful source of and force for revelation, they spring out of Jesus' perceptive observations of the world around him. However, an important issue needs to be faced. Were the parables and the other ways in which Jesus' insights about God are related to this world, only illustrations of revelation, a teacher's technique, or do they point to one of the ways in which truth came to him? Matthew 6.28 is a highly significant verse in helping to answer our question, "Look how the wild flowers grow". David Hill makes this comment on the word for look. "The Greek word *Katamantho* occurs only here in the New Testament; it implies careful study with a view to learning".[4]

Jesus clearly encouraged observation of the world around as a source of understanding of whom God is, although equally he recognized the need for God to reveal himself and his will, and the danger of obtuse blindness to what God revealed.

But Jesus not only directs his disciples to the "world of nature", but also to the world of ordinary people. It is true that the commitment, courage, care of the shepherd, and enthusiastic response at his success, is presented as a model divine experience. So, too, is the joy of a woman who has recovered her wedding dowry after a distressed and dusty search. But so also are the unjust steward who seeks to preserve his own neck in the pressure of his master's unexpected return, and the workers in the vineyard who grumble about unfair treatment, held up as pointers to the reality of God. This is true in very different ways. But it is all part of the fascination of discovering God's presence in our world through openness to it and to him. Jesus not only gains insight from the tranquillity and peace of the wild flowers on the Galilean hillside, but also from towers falling unexpectedly and undeservedly on Galileans. Both the world of nature and the world of work, both the restful and the violent, the beautiful and the ugly, can be a source, a catalyst for an encounter with God. The world does not determine the experience of God but it facilitates it.

Such worldly sources for his revelations are by no means the only ones. As the traditions are significant with the prophets, so with Jesus; God's revelations in the Scriptures are foundational. There is no such thing as scientific, objective observation for Jesus. He wears the spectacles of scriptural insight to focus the truth and to filter out the false. He views his world through a mind whose frames of reference and whose value systems are formed with the help of the Scriptures he knows so well, and the God to whom they bear witness. Yet, so frequent and pervasive are the direct contacts (as well as the hints and oblique references) with the world, it is difficult to dismiss the probability that facing the world provided Jesus with insight into the Kingdom.

If we move from the beginning to the end of the New Testament we also find support for our position, although it comes in a completely different way. In the book of Revelation chapters 2–3 are seven short letters given by the ascended Christ, through John to the angels of the seven churches in Asia Minor – Ephesus, Smyrna, Pergamum, Thyatira, Sardis, Philadelphia, and Laodicea. Each letter has a similar format but the content of each is very distinctive.

So often the content is related to the context of the specific city. Time and time again the message matches something significant about the places or the people or the history of the city. It is as though heavenly reality transcends the worldly. It may be difficult to establish that it is the observation of the distinctiveness of each city which has led to the revelation of God's message to each, but there is no doubt that it has influenced the shape and scope of each message.

R. Paul Stevens in an insightful article[5] would claim something similar for the rest of the Book of Revelation. His argument is that in Revelation, contemplation and the real world of John's day are "married".

> *Contemplation normally requires withdrawal from culture and politics... Contemplation makes us think of stillness; apocalypse makes us think of earth-shattering thunder and blinding light. Contemplation is closet-work; apocalypse is cosmos work.*

He continues:

> *Lay spirituality must deal not only with ecclesiastical life (Revelation 2–3) but with power, politics, economics, marketing and social responsibilities in secular or religious society. This John does. The stillness he seeks is not quietude but the triumphant voice of God... in the context of our conflict ridden life in this world... John accomplishes this by pulling back the curtain of "normal" perception to let us see a transcendent reality that is actually present in our everyday existence, to see through the eye, as Blake proposed, not merely with it.*

R.P. Stevens emphasizes that the apocalypse is concerned to help us experience God, not merely know about him, let alone know about the future course of history. John, then, is concerned to help us look at our world and to see through it to know God.

What we find then in Scripture, in a variety of places and certainly a variety of expressions, is an awareness that the context in which we live provides an opportunity for us to discover God's truth in a personal way which not only provides us with information about God, but which also brings the truth of God into our experience. Thus there is support for those who would encourage us to renew and discover our experience of God in the quietness, by patiently waiting before the natural world. Yet it pushes us much further, to a conviction that God strides upon and into the often noisy, muddled, chaotic, and strident world in which we now live.

Here then is our opportunity and challenge to venture outwards to our secular world, the whole of it, to take us upwards and onwards in our experience of God. But why do we need to practise this art, why do we need to learn openness to our world, and what are the advantages if we do?

Suggested Activities

1. Read through parts of the Book of Proverbs and try to perceive what experiences gave rise to the sayings – chapter 10 is a good starting point.

2. Look at one or more of the Gospels – see how often Jesus refers to ordinary events:

   - in parables

   - in his general conversation

   Consider, too, how ordinary everyday experiences provide opportunity for God's presence to be made clear, e.g. fishing (Luke 5.1–9), eating (Mark 2.13–17), a storm (Matthew 8.23–27), foot washing (John 13.3–17).

Notes

1   Brother Ramon writes, "By the grace and love of God, though the
     imago Dei, the image of God, has been broken and defaced, yet there
     are traces and echoes of the divine image within us. That means that
     the imagination of man, though it may be tainted, is also capable of
     intellectual truth and aesthetic beauty, for the Holy Spirit continues
     his creative work". This, I maintain is true not only for the
     imagination but for all that people produce as well! *Praying the
     Bible*, p. 21.

2   In other words either "experience" could have been triggered by
     human observation; either could have occurred in Jeremiah's mind
     without any immediate, specific, correlating observation.

3   T.R. Glover 1896–1943 – *Baptist Hymn Book* – A quotation from
     one of his books is worth noting. "His knowledge of God is not a
     matter of quotation as ours very often tends to be. He is conscious
     always of the real nearness of God..." *The Jesus of History* (London,
     1920), p. 92.

4   David Hill (New Century Bible) *The Gospel of Matthew* (London,
     1977), p. 144. Of course in Matthew 6.26 (look at the birds) the
     Good News Bible again says "look", but it is a different word,
     no doubt here with the same meaning.

5   R. Paul Stephens, "Poems for people in distress: The Apocalypse
     of John and the contemplative life" *Themelios*, Jan. 1993, vol. 18,
     no. 2, pp. 11–14.

4 WHY BOTHER?

In the most important sense this chapter cannot be written – it can only be experienced. The real justifications for any journey are the experiences on the way and even more the result of the stay. Yet a guide book or a holiday brochure has its place. Perhaps it encourages us to invest ourselves at all; without its allurement we would stay at home. Perhaps it adds to our journey, for it helps us look out for places of special interest and fills in some historical comments that enhance our appreciation. When we arrive it helps us plan effectively or tells us what to avoid because it does not interest us. All the while we are not only discovering the places but something about ourselves as well. Nevertheless, a guide book is a poor substitute for our own adventure. This is more than true in our case. But some delineation can help prepare us or maybe entice us!

Let us begin with Bill Hybels. Bill, you recall, was helpfully honest in admitting he does not always get an answer from God when he prays, and discerning enough to realize this may be because, for some reason, "God chooses to remain silent" (see Chapter 3). However, he is not naïve enough to place all the responsibility on God. He continues:

> *I know that God continues to speak to his people today, and I am convinced that there are two reasons we don't hear his voice more often. The most obvious reason is that we don't listen for it. We don't schedule times of stillness that make communication possible.*

This is perhaps of even greater significance than Bill allows for. Why do I say that? Well, let us ask a further question. Why don't we make times for God? One reason is that we find the television or the CD player more satisfying than God – we are more or less guaranteed some immediate and gratifying response and input from the machine. If we don't like it we can express our disappointment and our power by switching it off. God doesn't work like that – and maybe we wish he did; to await God means recognizing our dependence and choosing not to give ourselves immediate sensory gratification. Furthermore, our tendency to go for sensory gratification actually dulls our desire for God and may end our search. For the television doesn't ask us to go beyond itself – it is an end in itself. God always calls us beyond the observed and experienced to worship him alone.

Secondly, the television or CD does not make inherent demands on us, other than paying some kind of attention – although it is just as happy if we go to sleep! God calls us to attention, into a deepening relationship, on to a changed life, and a different pattern of behaviour. This does not sound like good news for tired people. Yet, according to God we've got this wrong.

Just as a tired, cold person can't be bothered to eat the warm meal placed in front of them, but that meal, once begun, will start to deal with the cold and tiredness, so Scripture says:

> *He strengthens those who are weak and tired.*
> *Even those who are young grow weak;*
> *young men can fall exhausted.*
> *But those who trust in the Lord for help*
> *will find their strength renewed.*
> *They will rise on wings like eagles;*
> *they will run and not get weary;*
> *they will walk and not grow weak.*

Isaiah 40.29–31

But finding the personal energy to turn from the television to God is not necessarily easy. It is safer, and superficially easier, to fill the space with other things than leave it open for the possible arrival of God; when he doesn't arrive we have the additional problem of disappointment to handle too and we all know how demotivating that can be.

Thirdly, the fact we don't make times of stillness available can be indicative of our disobedience and our rebellion. We don't really want God to speak because we can deceive ourselves into thinking we are not being disobedient! Our failure to be available is the primary example of our disobedience. No wonder God tells us that our sins cause a separation between him and us.

We need to face Bill's question "When do you make yourself quiet and available to God? When do you formally invite him to speak to you?" Please note what he says: "make *yourself* quiet and available". It is not primarily a question of our surroundings, but of ourselves. We can ask him to speak to us through whatever is impacting our senses – if we believe he can and wants to, and if we want him to.

But we are asked a second question. "In addition to carving out blocks of time to listen to God, do you keep your ears tuned to him each day?" In order to help us perceive more clearly what he has in mind Bill provides us with an insightful illustration. He writes as follows:

A friend of mine has a company car equipped with a radio, a cassette player, a phone and a mobile communication unit, which he monitors at a very low decibel level when he's in the car. Often we've been driving together, talking and listening to a tape, when all suddenly he'll reach down, pick up the microphone, and say I'm here, what's up?

With all the noise in the car, I never hear the mobile unit's signal. But he has tuned his ear to it. He is able to carry on a conversation without ever losing his awareness that a call may come over that unit.

For our purposes this is an even more telling challenge. Some people would not know the unit was there and that Bill's friend had the potential for receiving messages; they would only notice (if they did) the cassette, the conversation, and the traffic noise. Some, like Bill, know about the potential but still do not hear the tell-tale sign. Why not? Partly it is a matter of practice – of training our subconscious, or whatever the appropriate part of the brain, always to be alert. This does not mean a lessening of awareness and care for the driving, the music and the company, it is something extra. But partly it is also a matter of commitment. Bill's friend is more highly motivated to pick up the messages; he knows how important they are, though whether they are from his wife or his business, we are not told. Some way or other those messages are crucial; getting them is vital. Bill's friend knows how to live normally with an extra level of awareness. [1]

This is partly what we are wanting to achieve through our process of meditation – an ability to live in a constant (or at least more constant) openness to the possibility that God will speak to us, through all that is going on around us; a willingness, indeed a deep desire to hear him call, and then give him special attention so we can pick up his message to us and respond positively. Bill's illustration shows us that we need three things:

1. the potential medium of communication (including, of course, someone who wants to get through to us);

2. the practice which will help us pick up the "alert" signal;

3. the commitment to hear and respond by paying attention when the message comes through.

Much of this book is about point 2. Of course, it therefore presupposes 1 and to some extent 3. The "to some extent 3" is worthy of amplification. Like many other things in life our commitment grows as we come to see the value of something. We may not be very bothered about having a fire alarm system in our home; maybe it is just there when we buy the house; we have never thought of installing one before and probably wouldn't do so. However, suppose one night the fire alarm goes off because a fire has started in our house. This raises us from sleep and ensures the survival of the family. It also means there is only minimal damage to the house and furnishings. Then we suddenly have a much higher commitment to maintaining the alarm in good working order. Or, consider this situation. Perhaps hill walking has never appealed. Then, a friend persuades us to go with them; we do it more for the sake of friendship than anything else. However, it turns out to be one of those perfect days with crystal-clear viewing, magnificent autumn colours, stunning vistas stretching from horizon to horizon. By the end of the day it feels as though we have drunk in vast quantities of beauty and we have received a new kind of zest for living. To our amazement the scenes which have surprised and satisfied us come to our mind at the most unexpected moments, as we stare at the petrol filler nozzle, as we hang out the washing, as we mow the lawn. In so doing the freshness of that day recharges us. We find we have become hooked on hill walking. This is what I mean by "to some extent" – a willingness to try, to go along with someone or something, a freedom to allow ourselves to become enchanted with the possibility of meeting God in the most unexpected moments. I do not mean we must start with a passionate commitment that this is the best thing since...

However, the analogies above, particularly the second one, can be misleading. For some it may be "love at first sight" so to speak. For others it may be more like the long haul of learning a new language or mastering a musical instrument. Just as then we need to hold on to the future potential of the process (the freedom to communicate during an overseas holiday or the opportunity to play in an orchestra), in order to keep us going, so we may need to remind ourselves of the joyful privilege of a fresh experience of or even with God. It may therefore help to read again Chapter 2, or talk with friends, who can share with you the wonder of the time when they heard God calling to them through the routines of their lives.

We now have the first answer to the question "Why bother?" We bother because it is worth it. It is worth it because God is wanting to speak with us in all kinds of situations; worth it because we can learn to pick up his "alert" signals, worth it because the end result is worth it for us, for others and I dare to think for God himself.

However, there is another kind of level which needs to be addressed. Here, the issue is that we need to bother because "It is necessary if we are going to cope spiritually in our culture".

Geoffrey Maughan is vicar in Abingdon. He has written a most helpful article[2] about relating the Gospel to our culture. He has done this by elucidating the nature of our culture. He believes we have entered the period of post-modernity. That is, the domination of the scientific models of "knowledge" are losing their dictatorial powers.

The limits of scientific certainty are increasingly being felt. Transcendence is returning on to the stage of contemporary thought as something which is seen to be important though illusive... Christianity needs to recover a confidence in its own epistemological certainty... The model of "personal knowledge" is a thoroughly Christian epistemology which fully accepts the partial perspective of the "knower" without denying the validity of what he knows.

The details of the "how", "why", and "whether" of all that Geoffrey Maughan is saying need not concern us, but one of his observations is most important, for our purposes:

A further important feature of post-modernity is a pre-occupation with the visual image.

p. 4

Geoffrey recognizes that there are enormous dangers when the image is separated from reality but suggests, rightly, in my opinion, that this move towards the visual image, points to a way of knowing which is opportune and important for Christians to grasp.

How shall the gospel speak into this world of the surface image? First we can see that the gospel is full of images... and the Christians should have no hesitations about using these and a million other images in its presentation of the gospel... Secondly we believe that God has made his creation in a sacramental way... so that however much the contemporary person is concerned only with the superficial image, there will still be the opportunity for moments of disclosure which will open up the eternal reality beyond the surface image.

For our perspective, Maughan is claiming both that the world has the potential to speak to us of God, or that God can speak to us through it and that this is a particularly appropriate way for us "to know God" at this stage in our culture's development. We need to learn this way because other routes are being closed down, with long and difficult diversions and hold ups. Naturally, to leave the well-known highway has its own dangers, but also its benefits, highlights, and rewards, particularly in our culture.

The driving skills are different and the vehicle which has the edge on the motorway may not be so comfortable on mountainous terrain. There may well be a change in the priority of perceptions and abilities, which will be hard for both those who lose their leading position and for those who find to their surprise, that they are "in front" but are not trained for leadership. They may lack the confidence to distribute their learning, and equip others to follow and even surpass them. Nevertheless, if we are going to be able to perceive the Gospel for ourselves with full perspective and proclaim it with full conviction, we need to discern the voice of God through "the world" around *us* and not only the world of creation, as we have understood it. So the second kind of answer to the question "Why bother?" is that we need to because of the culture in which we live.

There is still a third kind of answer which needs to be considered. This relates not so much to our culture but to our capacities. It is the argument of Walter Wink in *Transforming Bible Study*[3] that we have attenuated that part of our total mental facility that most easily relates to insight that comes through the meditative approach. This is not at all unlikely. It is hard to develop an "athlete" to his perfection both for cycling and weight lifting at the same time. Different muscles need to be developed for the different sports, different mental attitudes, different kinds of co-ordination, and different skills are at a premium. So, if we have lived through a period which has emphasized the virtue of the analytical approach to issues, it is not surprising if, for many of us, the other side of our mental capacity has been underdeveloped and undervalued, just as if everyone trained for cycling and weight lifting had been despised and ignored. For the wholeness of a person necessary for normal life, there are values in developing muscles and co-ordination which allow us, as it were, both to cycle and lift weights. Equally in the spiritual realm we need to be able to function analytically and intuitively. But if the intuitive approach has been downgraded we may think that it is unimportant, illegitimate, or at least that we are not capable of it. In order to redress the balance we may need to concentrate on building the intuitive approach. We have seen this may be necessary for our culture; we now see it as necessary for us to be as rounded and complete as we can be.

We are now almost ready to embark on our journey of development to increase our ability to hear what God is saying to us through the world around us. I believe it is quite reasonable that if God finds we are listening to him in a certain way he will choose to speak more frequently that way. He wants to get through to us – this should surely encourage us. However, there is a warning I wish to give.

If we are convinced that it is worth bothering then we need to decide that we are willing to carve out time to learn to listen to God, to ask him to tune us into his signals, however strange this may seem at first. If we revert to the analogy of the athletes, then it is obvious that reading books or even watching videos on muscle building programmes will not, of itself, achieve much. *We need to do the exercises*. Sometimes they will be painful; then we still need to proceed, but obviously with some caution. Often we will need encouragement; frequently it is at the point when the athlete is giving up, that the breakthrough occurs. So it will be with the "build-up exercises" which follow. Hence, it is a significant advantage to work in a group, particularly with someone who really understands what it is all about. This is also a spiritual business and so it needs to be surrounded by prayer. So get other people praying for you. This process is about spiritual growth and awareness, so we should understand that the enemy will seek to sabotage our growth. Paul's advice applies here, as much as elsewhere.

> *Put on all the armour that God gives you, so that you will be able to stand up against the Devil's evil tricks. For we are not fighting against human beings but against the wicked spiritual forces in the heavenly world, the rulers, authorities, and cosmic powers of this dark age. So put on God's armour now! Then when the evil day comes, you will be able to resist the enemy's attacks; and after fighting to the end, you will still hold your ground.*

> *So stand ready with the truth as a belt around your waist, with righteousness as your breastplate.*

Ephesians 6.11–14

Suggested Activities

1. Are there situations where you seem more receptive than most people to what is going on around you? If so, why do you think this is? Is it aptitude, training, experience...? Might this have a transferable application for your sensitivity to God?

2. Think of a situation when you were desperate to communicate with someone: e.g. urgent telephone message – no answer; personal visit – no one in; talk to your boss or your minister about some crisis and they were unavailable. How did this make you feel – towards them, yourself, the situation? Did you leave a message to let them know you had called, or requesting they contact you? How do you think God feels when he cannot get through to us? When people you want are not there, do you ever think "I won't waste time on them again"? Could this affect your attitude to God?

3. Do you find it easier to work intuitively or analytically? Are you more suspicious of carefully argued positions or emotively presented ones? Why?

Notes

1   Compare Paul in Ephesians 6.18: "Pray on every occasion, as the spirit leads. For this reason keep alert". See *An Adventure in Prayer*, forthcoming.

2   "Issues of Gospel and Culture in Modern Secular Britain", *Ambassador*, July 1993, p. 1 p. 3.

3   London, 1981 – see especially Chapter 1.

DEVELOPING OUR AWARENESS OF GOD

Even as I start to write I am filled with self-questioning. I am painfully aware that if God is not there for us, no matter how sensitive and sensitized you may be or become, I can accomplish nothing and you will experience confusion not revelation, frustration and not fulfilment. So, I wonder if I should call this section "Developing our abilities to perceive God when he manifests himself", but somehow that makes it too person-centred, too human, too objectified. Yet, at the end of the day, we are in God's hands over this issue. I have some control over the directions in which I take you, the order in which I seek to develop your sensitivity, but I have no control over what you will find when you start to "look", even less over what you experience as you "look" and none whatsoever over what God will choose to say or what you will make of what he says. I feel somewhat like Jesus saying to his disciples "Get into the boat and go ahead to the other side of the lake" and then finding a storm has blown up – but unlike Jesus I feel I cannot control the storm! Nevertheless we must go forward.

If you have never spent time in meditation or a retreat, then the first chapter in this section may help you to get started. If you have, then you may want to move straight to Chapter 6.

5 CHRISTIAN MEDITATION – AN INTRODUCTION

In this chapter I have tried to gather together a small selection of the better known kinds of meditation to give you some kind of appreciation of this approach. It will help to alert us to some of the faculties within us which may have been dormant. It can serve as a kind of warm-up exercise before the main developmental process.

But first I want to explore a fundamental matter, that is, one which needs to be faced even before we start the preparation for meditation. It is this: "Isn't all this talk of awareness completely subjective? Aren't things, things, and that's an end of it? Isn't there an objective world of reality and the rest is subjective projection, in the end nothing more than fantasy?"

My answer to this is that there are many levels of significance which are based in reality and to be ignorant of them or their possibility and, perhaps even worse, to ignore them, is not to serve objectivity but falsely to limit it. Let me illustrate this by exploring a very simple issue – peeling potatoes!

Please understand that I am not claiming this section is "Christian Meditation". Rather it is an attempt to remove one of the very stubborn barriers which exists for many Western Christians. It is an attempt to introduce people to doorways through the brick wall of "objectivity", which are necessary to know about if we are to enjoy the reality of Christian Meditation. Otherwise we may mistake the wall for the extent of reality; rather than a barrier it is merely a boundary. It is not necessary that it imprisons our awareness of and appreciation of reality. So, come with me as I introduce you to some of the truth about my potato peeling.

Prior to sitting down to write this chapter I was standing at the kitchen sink peeling potatoes. That was the observable, objective fact – although no one was there to observe it – there was only me experiencing it. The rest of the family were still in bed. I could be resentful about that but I am not! I normally peel the potatoes on Sunday mornings and I do it not because I have to, but because I want to. It is a symbolic way of expressing my appreciation to my wife for the way she cooks for us most of the time. But why Sunday? Partly because I don't rush off to work in the same way as the rest of the week. But why not Saturday then? Well, I suppose it is because I want Sunday to be special for her; the reason for that is our Christian commitment and desire to follow the Scriptures in setting aside a day for worship – and yes I know a previous generation would have peeled them on Saturday night, so to that extent I am a child of my times, but peeling the potatoes helps free her and hopefully express my love. So the fact of my peeling the potatoes cannot be understood properly without appreciating a great deal about my life values, my commitment to my wife, and our commitment to God.

I have already touched on another dimension of the issue. We have a family of three children. On Sundays particularly they all have large appetites, so we need to peel a lot of potatoes! Hence, it is more of a task than might at first be thought. If we didn't have a family, I might well not be peeling the potatoes but doing something else, vacuuming for instance.

However, the choice of tasks to help and express my love may well involve other factors. For some reason there is for me a tactile satisfaction in peeling potatoes – the warm water, holding the potatoes in my large hands, so they nestle there, but can easily be manoeuvred. I have a facility for peeling them. It's a small insignificant matter, anybody can do it, but then you see I don't have great levels of manual dexterity; from their size you would expect I could have craftworker's hands but I don't and wish I did. So actually doing a manual task well gives me a quiet kind of satisfaction. I find it soothing, standing there, alone, with time to think as well as work. Probably if I had arthritis in my hands I would not be doing it either.

So, somewhere down the line I learnt this skill, mainly from my mother. I can still see her there, standing in our kitchen, although strangely the memory is more of her peeling apples – the long, wriggly, snakelike peelings. Yet it was through her encouragement, patience, and the opportunity she allowed me that I learnt. Peeling potatoes is part of my family history. Maybe that is also why I am doing this job.

But there are other equally valid dimensions to this simple issue. If you watched me you would see I use two knives that are very different. One is light and plastic – a dual-purpose knife – a peeling blade which can be inverted to reveal a single blade. I only use the peeling blade. We have used this particular design for many years.

When it eventually breaks, we always look for another. We cannot find a design to equal it. The steel stays sharp. The twin peeling blade is free to move and follow the contours of the potatoes, making the job much easier, quicker, and satisfying. When it breaks we try the other knife we have, but it isn't the same. That dual-purpose knife represents hundreds of years of human technical achievement – the development of steel, the discovery of plastic, design, and ergonomics; international relationships are also included because it is imported from another European country. It is such a simple thing – it probably represents the peak of achievement – for the design has stayed the same for nearly twenty years. It is light, convenient, and colourful; what is more important it works. It represents someone's job, a marketing system, a stable commercial world and much more. It is available for me. All of this is part of the truth of why I am peeling the potatoes the way I do.

But I only use the peeler, not the other blade, so why? The reason is because the other knife is used for cutting the potatoes and removing the "bad bits". The other knife is quite different in every way, in feel, design, history, and personal significance. It too is well designed for its functions. It will probably last our lifetime out. The blade is stronger, and thicker. The handle is wooden and there are three dominant brass rivets fixing the handle to the blade. It too works well. But we did not buy it. It was one of a pair of knives; the other is a large meat knife. They arrived one Christmas time from America, so it is not surprising they were "made in Chicago". They were sent by my wife's older sister and are valued not only for themselves but because we don't often receive gifts from her. Not that there is a relational problem but rather they have rarely had enough money to send presents. So these knives represent a better time in their financial history and that gives them a good feel too. But why is my sister-in-law in the USA? Because she married an American serviceman who was based in England in the aftermath of the Second World War and returned to America with him after they were married.

Peeling potatoes the way I do it involves the history of "civilization" in the twentieth century. It also involves the birth of Christ and the plan of God – for the knives came as a Christmas present. All of this lies in my hand when I peel a potato. It is all part of the truth, the reality of the situation. Already the simple act of peeling potatoes proves to have links with a very wide range of human experiences. But there is still more to gain from this example.

For, there's not only the tools, there are the potatoes! We bought them by the sackful and we bought them from a particular shop, attached to a garden centre on the A45. It was in fact the second sack we bought from that shop. The first I bought because it was convenient and I saw the sign. This particular sack was purchased because the first potatoes seemed so good and my wife wanted another sack from there. I can remember when we bought them. We had been to Luton to visit my wife's stepmother and the return journey was a convenient opportunity to get them. The shop is way out of Coventry, where we live, on one side of a dual carriageway. So behind the purchase of those potatoes is another family story of bereavement, and joy, and renewed bereavement. Behind it is the powerful pull of relationships, perhaps even the command "to honour your father and mother". Behind it too is the decision of the garden centre to sell things like potatoes. I have no knowledge of that decision, but it seems unlikely to me that the garden centre grew them themselves. Is the supplier a friend or relative of the owner? Did they decide to sell vegetables to encourage motorists on to their premises in the hope that once having stopped they would tend also to buy the plants and flowers which are their real *raison d'etre*? I don't know what the truth is but someone's decision made it possible.

And someone grew these potatoes. Land is owned or rented; people and machinery are used and managed. The development of seeds, the fight against disease, the nature of the soil where these potatoes were grown have all contributed to the simple act of peeling these potatoes, with their specific shapes, each one different, even if they are within certain parameters because of the specific variety. If Sir Walter Ralegh had not brought them back from America... or whatever the explanation of the bringing of potatoes here is, I would not have been peeling them, and if I did not have the desire to help people maximize their openness to God in our modern world, you would never have known that I peel the potatoes on Sunday mornings, particularly this Sunday morning.

All of this is, in different ways, part of the reality. What appeared a very simple procedure with little significance viewed as a general routine activity carried out by millions of people every day, becomes a much more complex event with links in all kinds of directions, touching some of the most significant happenings in Western history, some of the most profound concerning personal relations, and some of the fundamental values of the Christian faith. All these layers, interweaving, reflecting, revealing are legitimately part of the truth. Why should it seem strange then if God too can be present in the complex reality? Indeed he is, not only in the ways indicated but many more too, from his presence in the creative process of growth, through to his wisdom being gleaned and applied by science and technology, and to my personal history and encounter with him. But he might also have more personal things to show us of himself through this or any other experience that comes our way.

What I have tried to show in this investigation of potato peeling is that there are many levels of truth and reality with respect to even the most simple human experience. While science may concentrate on what is common to such experiences, personal awareness can legitimately investigate what is distinctive with some surprises on the way, including a realization that God, too, is there for us. Such observations are not to be confused with fantasy or imagination which is in a completely different category. What I have described is part of the objective truth.

But, I would have missed much of it had I not taken time to enter into the experience of doing it. It's there all right, but not always at the level of my consciousness, and that is where learning to meditate comes in. It is not about fantasy, it is about truth. Truth which is shaping my life and impacting the environment, but often the kind of reality of which I am unaware.

Here is a simple experiment to help you test out what I am claiming in the *audible realm*. It is even more impressive if you do this with other people but it can be done on your own. The basis of it is that much of the time we do not hear many of the sounds going on around us; we probably don't need to, we can't listen to everything at once, we have to be selective in order to respond to the sounds which are significant, but they are nevertheless part of reality.

So, give yourself time. Find a comfortable but not soporific chair and take a few deep breaths, not straining but gradually relaxing. It often helps to rest your hands gently on your thighs – but what is comfortable for you is what really counts. When you feel relaxed and ready, start to take note. What can you hear outside the house, especially the things you might not have noticed – maybe the songs of birds, maybe cars, lorries, motorbikes rushing along in the distance, perhaps a siren – do you know whether it is police, fire, ambulance, or a paramedic ambulance? Maybe you can hear footsteps or voices, an aeroplane or helicopter, maybe dogs barking or children playing. It could even be footsteps approaching your door – is it a familiar sound or footsteps you don't recognize – or do you not know the distinctive sound patterns that people make? Perhaps you can hear the wind – blowing through what?

After, say, ten minutes change the focus of your listening. What can you hear inside the building, within your house but outside the room you are in? Can you hear the central heating system, footsteps overhead, someone laughs or sneezes – a click as a light goes on or off, the oscillating noise of a fluorescent tube, the freezer engine starts up, or the washing machine spins? Perhaps your quietness is interrupted by angry voices in the adjacent semi-detached house, or the next flat.

When you sense you have learnt to listen to all the sounds outside the room you are in, listen to the sounds within your room. Really be prepared to take time on this one, although by now you can probably tune in much quicker. To start with you may not think there is much to listen to, but wait patiently – you can hear the normal breathing of other people, the self-adjustment of a floorboard, the creak of a chair, the rub of cloth on cloth, the squeak of a shoe moving as someone changes their foot position.

Finally, listen to the sounds within you. The level of your breathing, the noises within your ears, the sound caused by the moving of your hair, swallowing, your digestive system, your physical movements, however slight, are causing sounds – the adjustment of your jaw, your tongue rubbing on your teeth...

Perhaps you only managed to "listen" to these different environments with considerable effort and patience. Probably at some time or other your emotional frustration made things even harder. Just imagine then how difficult it is to listen to all these levels of sound at once. But that is only one of the problems we have. If one sound irritates us or triggers fear it may well block out for us many other sounds. We contribute enormously to what we hear and don't hear. So, now relive the processes you have just been through, and try and "recover" your responses to what you heard, and reflect on how they may have hindered or even helped the hearing process.

So much of what we could hear we don't listen to. This is true of the sounds around us and it is also true of the human voice. One value in learning to listen like the exercise above, is that we can transfer the skill to listening to people in a new kind of way, so that we start to hear the tone of voice and understand their message – to recognize the hidden anger, pain, or puzzlement. Their choice of just "those words" provides us with a clue to how to proceed and a new quality enters our relationship.

But a new quality of listening can help us become aware of God too. Why not read some of the Scriptures listed below, better still tape-record them or get someone else to read them for you as you listen, or best of all do this as a small group exercise, each reading one of the passages in turn. Whichever way you do it, please take your time, don't rush, let the words sink deep into your being and learn to listen to God with a new kind of alertness; one that is born not so much out of intensity but out of a restful sensitivity.

- Genesis 3.8–13 (you will need verses 1–7 for the context.)
- 1 Samuel 3.1–5, 6–9, 10–14, 15–17

Leave three to five minutes between sections and try to understand how time contributed to the experience.

- Psalm 98.1–3, 4–6, 7–9
- Pause between each section
- Matthew 4.18–20; 9.1–2; Mark 4.39–40; 5.38–42

Listen carefully to Jesus.

- John 3.5–9
- Acts 2.1–6

Someone wrote to me today – the day after writing this section – telling me of a church leaders' weekend and commented "Saturday was a good time; God spoke to us – and I was quite overcome by that alone – the Living God, who created the universe – spoke to *us*!"

He is speaking to us today. Scripture gives us this invitation and assurance:

> *Come, let us bow down and worship him; let us kneel before the Lord, our Maker! He is our God; we are the people he cares for, the flock for which he provides. Listen today to what he says.*

> Psalm 95.6–7

Jesus adds:

> *The man who goes in through the gate is the shepherd of the sheep. The gatekeeper opens the gate for him; the sheep hear his voice as he calls his own sheep by name... the sheep follow him, because they know his voice.*

> John 10.2–4

So, we can ask God to teach us to listen to his voice among all the other noises of the day.

Our adventure into audible alertness has shown us that we can miss many sounds, perhaps because at a subconscious level they do not seem important to us. Yet, we have discovered we have the capacity to tune into many more messages than we would normally register. In a parallel way we can miss so many of the messages God is giving to us, even when we are listening to Scripture. Just as we can develop a capacity to "hear" more than we normally do, so, with God's help, we can learn to hear him more, more clearly and with greater immediacy, and this not only through Scripture but through events and experiences as well.

VISUAL

Candles have traditionally played a significant part in Christian worship; they are making a comeback in some Free Churches and in the field of Christian Meditation. I have several significant memories of candles, which I wish to share with you, not for you to remain with my memories, although you may if you wish, but to trigger off your own recollections.

When I was a child we would visit my maternal grandmother. She lived in a mining town in Derbyshire. The air smelt of coal, the apple tree was coated in the dust, somehow integrated into the rough bark. In my early years the downstairs rooms were lit by gaslight, but we made our way to bed as small children by candle-light. I remember with some fear, the flickering light and the leaping shadows which the flame, vulnerable to the many draughts which galloped and gulped from every nook and cranny, projected all around me. The candle for me was not the comfort it is to many, it was the death knoll on a day, the eerie journey to a cold bed, and the uncertain moments or hours before sleep overtook me.

Another memory is of my first pastorate in Leicestershire. The time was the "winter of discontent". Candles became a highly valued commodity, part of the necessary survival kit for the electricity blackouts, which stunned the town like a hard blow to the head, suddenly pulling down the blinds on visual awareness, disorientating street and home, destroying the normal pursuit of television viewing and causing all kinds of uncertainties in the domestic routine. A candle gave light, surrounded by pools of darkness, not only in the room, but in the society of which we were a part – itself on the edge of a mining community – inconvenience, violence, anarchy – where would it end – and all we had was a candle which would soon have burnt itself out.

The last slide I wish to project is very different. It is a brilliant, bright, sunny day in Jerusalem. The intense light is more vivid still because of the limestone walls and outcropping rocks. A few of us have, moments before, paid our fee to the keeper of the entrance of Hezekiah's tunnel, and he hands to each of us a candle, only slightly thicker than a pencil. As we approach the entrance and light the candle its insignificant flame seems an utter nonsense in the light of day – why do we bother with it? How stark the contrast when 40 metres into the tunnel and now, with sometimes our knees and sometimes our thighs, immersed in cold water, we make our way through the narrow crevice with several hundred metres of hard rock tunnel ahead of us. Now our only source of light is the whispering flame of the slight candles – amazingly they are enough – reflections from the water and even the rock face, polished by the brushing of a million pilgrims, comfort us and warm the deep darkness with hope and direction. At one point, where the shaft into the city protrudes into the tunnel, the candles were blown out. Never has darkness seemed so black – never a trickle of light more valued as we manage to ignite the wick and protect it with our cupped hands. That tiny light is enough to light our way and to read the amazing and historically significant inscription where the two teams of workers, one from inside and one from outside the walls, met: "This is the day of the boring through: whilst the miners lifted the pick each towards his fellow and whilst 3 cubits yet remained to be bored through there was heard the voice of a man calling his fellow, for there was a split in the rock on the right hand and on the left hand. And on the day of the boring through the miners struck each in the direction of his fellow" (*Interpreters Dictionary of the Bible*, Nashville, 1962, vol. 4, p. 354). To stand where they stood, to be amazed as they were amazed – for them the magic moment of encounter with each other, the flow of air through the tunnel cooling sweaty dusty faces, the certainty of a task almost completed – for us the magic of a meeting with history, the sound of Assyrian soldiers rushing from the history books into our today and the knowledge of a journey half-completed as we moved forward beyond the half-way mark. Without a candle we would not have made our way, without a candle we would not have seen the message and relived the excitement of the archaeologists who discovered it, as well as the workers who carved it.

Why not use a candle and invite God to share your journey? Perhaps the first step will be to buy one – will you buy a religious candle, an ordinary old-fashioned candle, or one of the beautiful, decorative, scented candles? The choice is yours, but the choice may affect your journey!

In what and where will you place it? To make this experience richer, it may help if there is a small group of you. Sometimes it helps to set the candle in the middle of the room with the lights dimmed and, if necessary, the curtains drawn. Sit comfortably and relax, then quietly light the candle. Try not to come armed with a battalion of texts, try not to insist on your expectations – indeed you may need to spend the first few minutes letting go of them, reaching a point often of disappointment, becoming more and more sure that nothing will happen, before you are ready for God to use this simple visual image to call things to mind, to call them up from the deep recesses of your mind, to journey through the tunnels of your memories, or, if he chooses, to pale the candle into insignificance by the brilliance of his own light. Be willing for nothing, value each little image and insight which comes, but don't prize too highly what you experience. This is above all a time for God to move into your awareness, as he wills. He knows what we need, he knows for what we are ready, he knows where he will take us. It is sufficient that we have chosen to give him time, our time, to give back to him with openness the time he has given first to us. It may be memories, verses, visions, reflections, or simply a candle in a room that we "see". Let it be enough for now. Don't strive to keep what comes – rather experience it. Too much attention on keeping will mean we lose the next moment, or indeed the present one.

After the agreed time, whether ten minutes or an hour (often it is better to start with a shortish period), give yourselves a few minutes to return, gradually start to recollect what you experienced, and if you are part of a group you may wish to share, at least, some of what you recollect. Often people find God is giving them an insight which is more for another than themselves – but in doing that he is giving them something very precious indeed, the privilege of being a divine messenger, and the experience of deep community being built.

TACTILE

Our sense of touch is also a gift which can become a channel through which God communicates. Some people are amazingly gifted in this respect – I am not, although, when I am needing to leave home early and therefore get dressed in the dark so as not to disturb my wife, I do amaze myself at the ability to know which trousers are which from the feel of the cloth. Those who are visually impaired often become very capable in this realm. How amazing to be able to read, and to do it so fluently, through those little raised dots, which most of us would hardly notice, let alone be able to recognize and interpret the configurations. Often it is helpful to begin this kind of meditation by closing our eyes, so that, like a person who is blind, we can concentrate on a faculty we normally disregard.

There are two main stages in the following exercise. The first is to encourage you to believe you can learn far more through your fingers than you thought. The second starts to develop the connection between our ability and things God may want to say to us.

Stage 1   Gather together a number of objects and place them in a bag, so that they are not visible to you. You may also want to blindfold yourself, or at least close your eyes. Then simply reach into the bag and grasp an object. First see if you think you can identify what it is. Now see how much you can discover about it through touch. Do you begin to appreciate it in a different kind of way? What do you notice about it you hadn't bothered with before? Size, structure, materials, sharp edges, softness, comfort in your hand, warmth, coldness etc. are some of the many features – but probably there will be a sense of something qualitative happening to your appreciation of it. When you have explored and enjoyed it place it on a table. Keep the various objects in order so you can check your views against reality.

Obviously this is more fun and interesting as a group exercise. There can be more of an element of surprise and discovery (although you can always ask someone else to gather your objects and put them in the bag for you to achieve this effect). But even more fascinating can be the sharing afterwards of what you notice and the learning of how much you didn't notice but someone else did!

Stage 2 Choose a pebble – perhaps pick one out from a group you have collected on the seashore or go out into the garden and find a few. Then, as with the candle, finding a comfortable, quiet and restful place, take your pebble in your hands. Hold it in all kinds of ways – let it lie on your hand, explore its shape with your fingers, squeeze it tightly in the palm of your hand, grip it with your finger ends, rub it on the back and front of your arm, along your fore-head, cheek, back of your neck, place it under your foot etc. Do this as often and for as long as you want – but be prepared to stay with it in any one or more of these experiences. Be ready to receive whatever comes to mind. This simple tactile experience may open a hundred channels to God. I don't know what he may say to you.

So, we have now tried three fairly traditional approaches to meditation. "What is going on?", we may well ask. First, we are re-educating ourselves by seeking to enliven our capacity to experience through our non-verbal communication channels. Hopefully this will increase our confidence in these areas, and encourage us to develop our sensitivity even more. Behind this is a belief that God can choose to communicate with us as he wills, through any aspect of his world and through any of the senses he has given us. He is *not* restricted to the verbal sphere alone. Second, using our other senses taps into a different aspect of our total memory bank, releasing memories into our present consciousness which may for a long time have been locked away from us, like works of art in a bank vault. These memories may prove to be a powerful resource for our living, but also, like those works of art, have a significant message we have missed – and probably a message from God. Third, many of our reflections will resonate with God's revelation in Scripture. This is not merely mental dittography for at least two reasons. First we may notice passages which before seemed irrelevant. Second there may well be a qualitatively different impact between "the word" and "the listener" because the message is conveyed by a different channel, and to a different and sometimes more significant place in our brain. Often this gives to it a capacity to influence our behaviour, our response mechanisms, or our character in a more effective way.

So we have made a start; entering into some of the riches which a more traditional approach to meditation brings, but it is now time for us to move on along our pathway to meditating in our modern world. As we go, however, I want to alert you to two other skills which may prove to be a great asset for your concern. These are the use of active involvement with our world and imaginative reflection on Scripture.

6 INTERACTION AND IMAGINATION

In Chapter 5 we attempted to receive messages from God through our environment using our senses of hearing, sight, and touch. We did this on the analogy that just as there are many "physical" sounds which don't register in our conscious minds, or "body language" messages we are not alert to, so with God, there may be many comments, insights, or even directives, that God may be communicating to us, but we miss them. But God is a God who works within us and with us, as well as communicating to us. It seems reasonable therefore that he can, should he so choose, get through to us as we engage in creative activity with the materials of his world. To be honest, this is an aspect of openness with which I have little personal experience.

I cannot draw or paint, although I can appreciate other people's work and creative abilities. I cannot write music or play any musical instrument, although music has a profound effect on my life, and is important both for expressing and creating the tones of my emotional being. I cannot sculpt or make clay pots, but I can admire people who do and can be helped or challenged by their work. Using a camera is a chore and normally I get it wrong, underlining an innate sense of incompetence with things technical and creative. However I have no problem whatever in accepting that there are people who can not only use natural materials but also express what they are perceiving in the natural world through their creative work. Such people have enormous opportunity for experiencing God by means of their creative activities.

Equally I can accept and welcome the possibility of such awareness of God, because it seems to me to be scripturally affirmed. This is no time for a complete "theology of the arts", but one or two pointers may serve us well. So, let us go back to the fundamentals.

> Then God said, "And now we will make human beings; they will be like us and resemble us. They will have power over the fish, the birds, and all animals, domestic and wild, large and small." So God created human beings, making them to be like himself.

Genesis 1.26–27

Here we see God acting creatively to express his own reality –
human beings are the results. But like the picture of a bottle of
Camp coffee on the Camp coffee label, there is here the potential
for almost infinite reproduction even if it is on an ever-decreasing
scale. If human beings are made in the image of a creative God,
then in being creative they are fulfilling the purpose for which they
are created. Both the process and the results are potentially an
expression of their likeness to the creative God, and hence a
source of God's revelation of himself. We must add "potentially"
because Genesis 3 tells of the Fall, of our rejection of that complete
willingness to release our creator's image in us, and our desire
to dominate the scene with our own destructive and detrimental
choices. Yet the image, although marred, has not been totally
obliterated, in human beings or the creative process.

I have no problem, then, in accepting this potential of creative
interaction with our world as a means of encounter with God,
because I can sometimes experience it second-hand through
meditation on the products of artistic activity, whether through
music, painting, carving, or whatever. If the product has the potential
for God to use, I am sure the process also has. Indeed I suspect it has
very powerful possibilities in this area, which may have been God's
main intention for it. When Paul came to Athens and saw the altar,
the result of an artist's active interaction with his world, it became a
source of revelation and proclamation. If something dedicated to
Paganism can be reclaimed by God and "restored", what is there to
stop him reinvading almost anything (Acts 17.16–31)?

A further reason for accepting the potential of artistic
expression, as a source of deep communication with God, is that
many people with the gift would bear witness to its power. Indeed
centres are now opening which seek to enhance this active
response, this integration of senses with the world, as a basis for
retreats and meditation.

Indeed, I recognize that through self-expression, whether in
flowers or stone, music or cookery, something of the self we
express may surprise us. We can explain it like this. Whatever it is
we make, acts like the image we see in a mirror. The "self" which
we have expressed through our activity, may give us a glimpse of
the God who made us. So I would encourage all who have gifts in
this area to explore them as a means of meeting God. Perhaps they
could spare me a prayer or two as well, asking God that one day I
may have the courage to venture into this realm – I'm sure it will
be for my healing!

Much of the insight from the realm of human arts and crafts applies to our working life as well. When Genesis talks about people being made in God's image, there is a link with God's directive that people "will live all over the earth and bring it under their control" (Genesis 1.27). In naming the animals and birds and cultivating the garden people are fulfilling their God-given image too. So, work as well as creative and artistic expressions are a legitimate focus for our attention. As I think and write I often have a sense of being with God and I am frequently surprised by the outcome. I sense sometimes that, in spite of me, God's thoughts are coming through. The same can be true in many areas of work. When a civil engineer designs a bridge, and a vast number of people co-operate to turn the design into reality, God's creative image is at work. It is not uncluttered, of course; so it is no wonder that the results, as with my writing, may be opaque to the presence of God rather than a completely clear representation of his image. But the point remains that both in the process as well as in the result there is the opportunity for openness to God. The same will be true whenever people are involved in using their God-given talents, whether it is producing a CD, designing an advertisement, building a house, preparing meals, or inputting data on to a computer. Some tasks are more opaque than others – both because the processes involved can be dehumanizing and the products alien to God (the arms industry for instance). Yet, we must be cautious in dismissing any area of human activity too quickly. Just as an imperfect flower may say as much or more to us than a perfect one, or a dead sparrow could speak to Jesus of God's care, so the same is true within the arena of work. Perfection is not required before God can be present.

Although there are times when I regret my lack of artistic ability or even manufacturing competence I am not too sad, for God has blessed me with another equally valuable and valid way of responding to and interacting with his world – it is the gift we call imagination. I would want to distinguish between imagination and fantasy, although I gladly recognize that we eventually run out of words, just as we run out of land if we drive east too far beyond Norwich! I would call *The Lion, the Witch and the Wardrobe* a work of the imagination – for it is dealing in truth, even though the story may be pure C.S. Lewis. Fantasy is what we dream up to escape from truth, to satisfy our egos and desires. Imagination enables us to arrive at, express, and receive what is true, in a way that bypasses our normal deductive processes. It has this similarity to art and music. If in our normal thinking we move steadily up a slope, then in art and music we climb up steps, and with imagination in one leap we may reach the top. The destination in terms of truth may be the same but the processes can be different. The processes are not thereby rendered insignificant, nor is one to be valued more than others. While the destination is vitally important, and of no place is this more true than when our destination is "in God", the varied process themselves have powerful possibilities as a way through which God may meet us.

Using or releasing our imaginative, intuitive abilities is probably a high risk activity, but I think a necessary, or at least valuable, asset on our journey of discovery. The risks are high because here more than anywhere we run the danger of creating God in our image. Among the reasons for this is the fact that imagination is not limited by the boundaries of the created materials with which the artist must work. Yet learning to handle this danger will equip us well for spotting the smaller but still serious risk of doing this with other approaches. In spite of the risks this too is an avenue which it seems has the validation of Scripture. For visions and dreams, so frequently the source of meeting with and message from God in both the Old and New Testaments, clearly depend on the same kind of faculties which we call imagination. Maybe, just because our imaginations are so flexible, they can be more available to God, more so perhaps than the disciplined processes of rational thought which may have ruled God out before the start, or even the creative fabrication of the artist, whose expressions are limited by materials, abilities, environment, and training.

In order to minimize the risks of imagination running wild, but also to gain confidence in the surrender of our imaginations to God, I invite you to share in one of the following biblical meditations. This approach was something I developed first in a pastoral context with a very clear sense that it was given to me by God. I then went on to apply it in group contexts, discovered that many people were helped by it, and entered into new awareness of God's reality. Only then did I discover that, in essence, it was an approach with a long history and a name "the Ignatian approach".

I normally divide the process of imaginative Bible encounter into four main sections which I describe using the acronym FIER (pronounced "fire"). This is how to unpack the initials:

- Familiarization
- Identification
- Experience
- Review

We shall unpack what these mean very soon but there is also a prologue and an epilogue, so to speak. The epilogue we will leave until after the explanation, but the prologue warrants our attention now.

The prologue consists of two main points. The first needs to happen before we ever use this approach to the Bible, and concerns our attitudes to the Bible and our imagination. If we think there is only one way to handle the Bible, and that is through the deductive part of our minds, applying them as we might to a text book on philosophy or chemistry with help from the Holy Spirit, then it will not be easy to handle the method I am now describing. However, I hope the following may help. First, Scripture is not all of one kind; there are laws, songs, stories, history, prophecy, genealogies. It is worth asking whether it is likely that one mind-set is going to be appropriate for such varied materials. Second, it is a maxim of properly interpreting the Scriptures that we must seek to understand the message as originally intended. Communication theory makes it clear that an important element is how the hearer receives the message or at least was expected to receive it. Can we assume that Moses' hearers or Isaiah's hearers or Jesus' hearers or Paul's hearers were dominated by a mind-set which originates in the seventeenth and eighteenth centuries, which we now refer to as the Enlightenment? If not, then we need to be cautious in thinking that our rational approach will reveal all the truth which was originally conveyed. Third, Jesus himself makes it clear that a mechanistic approach to Scripture will not allow us to grasp its living message. This was his criticism of the Pharisees (e.g. John 5.38–40). Perhaps our rationalistic approach, even when sensitized by the Spirit indwelling our mind, runs into similar dangers. Fourth, Jesus appeals to the imaginative faculties of his hearers and as his parables so clearly show, does not necessarily want to leave his people with fixed conclusions; he hoped for his continuing engagement with his hearers as their imaginative faculties sought to resolve or tease out the implications of his stories. The same is true for the "parable" of his whole life.

This is not to imply that the Bible is nonsense or that we don't need our deductive minds. Rather it is simply an attempt to create the space for people really to try the approach I am suggesting. Maybe, before being ready to "have a go", some people will require a few days or even weeks to talk this through with God. As I have considered the issues, the following is a brief statement of the position I have reached.

The Holy Spirit can reveal God's message from his Word through our intuitive faculties as well as our intellectual ones. Such an approach has certain advantages and some disadvantages; strengths and weaknesses might be preferable words. Among the advantages are that it helps a different group of people to those who operate more rationalistically. Second, the use of it claims, and has the potential for, cleansing our intuitive nature, thus helping to bring it under the Lordship of Christ. This is a very necessary process when so much advertising etc. is pulling at and probably polluting our intuitive person. Third, I believe this approach helps us develop our sensitivity to God and to one another, rather than only our under-standing. This seems significant for a faith which emphasizes relationships. Fourth, for most of us, it probably has a greater motivational power. By this I mean that if we see truth this way we are more likely to do something about it; truth gleaned this way has already made the journey from the head to the heart; it only needs to reach the hands and feet – a 12-inch drop!

Among the disadvantages are that it is less doctrinal and objective. It is less satisfying for those who are more logically orientated (although for such people there can be a special joy and release in finding they too can benefit from this approach). It is less of a corporate experience, although this needs to be qualified. For instance, no matter how biblical, cohesive, and teaching orientated the sermon might be, different people will hear different parts of it. If psychologists are right and we only "hear" 10 per cent of what is spoken, then there is considerable room for variation in what is actually communicated. As we shall see there are also ways of using FIER to bring in a corporate dimension. Finally, it requires greater personal participation. Whether this is a disadvantage is a debatable point! The concern might be that people would opt out, either mentally or physically. However, there is no guarantee that they are not so doing with other learning opportunities! This approach can be presented in a very non-threatening way, which leaves people free to participate at their own level. My own experience suggests that this concern is not a major threat.

The second preliminary consideration within this prologue relates more directly to "practical" steps we need to take. Whether we are working on our own or leading a group, we need to select a passage appropriate for this style (see the end of this chapter for a few suggestions) and most importantly we need to pray. We need to pray that God will quieten our bodies, minds, emotions and spirit, and that he will encourage us with a sense of his nearness, love, and desire to reveal himself to us. We may need to take quite a while for this part of the overall approach, especially if we are not used to the more meditative ways of interacting with Scripture.

THE PROCESS

Probably the minimum time requirement for this is 45 minutes to an hour.

1. Familiarization

In this phase it is important to remember our over-riding aim. Our intention is to let God speak to us through a passage of Scripture, not merely to "meditate". Therefore the content and significance of the passage are important; so is the context. The process of familiarization will certainly include reading the passage through in a variety of ways, for instance scanning the whole passage, reading a paragraph and letting it sink in, reading aloud, getting someone to read it to us, listening to our reading of it on a tape recorder. It may also be valuable to look at a few different translations. If it is a Gospel story which occurs more than once then we can gain different nuances by comparing the accounts. There is also plenty of room in this process for consulting commentaries and Bible dictionaries, although much of this is best done before we come to the time of meditation. The important point is that we want to be "comfortable" with the passage, able to recall its progress, not bewildered by an obscure word or custom, not side-tracked by an issue, but equally not so engrossed with our detailed knowledge that we cannot respond to the whole passage. If I am leading a group I would normally do careful preparatory work a few days before the meditation and I would experience the meditation for myself the day before.

2. Identification

Our aim here is to find someone in the story with whom we can identify, so that we can perceive the events from their perspective. Again, this is not an automatic mechanical process, but one in which we invite God to play his part. I do this by asking the Holy Spirit to lead us to the person that he wants to use to help us. Equally, it needs to be said it is not such a spiritual process that we can't contribute to it. There are many ways to find out who we are to be. We can ask ourselves, "Which person am I drawn towards?" This is one way in which God can be linking us with that person because we are in some way in a similar situation, have similar needs, or indeed recognize ourselves to be a similar kind of person. If this doesn't happen immediately or clearly then we can "focus down". The way I do this is to picture the scenes that I have been reading or hearing and then ask myself from what perspective I am seeing things.

For instance, if it is the story of the healing of the paralytic (Mark 2.1–12 etc.), is it from inside the house or outside the house, is it from the top of the roof or looking upwards? Is it from the front of the house alongside Jesus, or is it from the back of the room etc.? If it is the story of the woman with precious ointment (Luke 7.36–50), was it from the perspective of those sitting at the table, or from those looking on? Having settled on the perspective from which I am viewing things, I would then try and discern more specifically whom I was. If I was seeing things from the roof, was it as a spectator, one of the four friends, or the man being carried? If from outside the house, was it as a child, or a mother, or a pharisee – how much could I see? One important thing to realize in this part of the process is that there are nearly always people around in the story who hardly get a mention. For instance in the case of the paralytic, there were the people who owned the house. In the case of Jesus, at Simon the Pharisee's home, there would be those who had prepared and were now serving the meal, there were the disciples, and all kinds of other guests. Having decided I was, let us say, one of the four friends on this occasion, I might ask which one – did I originate the process of going, was I carrying the bed near the head or feet? If I were a disciple enjoying the meal with Simon, which disciple was I?

If this still does not lead us to sense some kind of identity it doesn't matter. We can simply "decide" to be someone. I do not think even this will be an arbitrary choice for we have asked God to help us! If we are leading a group and people still can't own a person we can make the choice for them. Again I believe we can trust God to help us in this process. His Spirit can guide us.

In all of this there are a few points worth noting. First, as we already indicated there are usually more people around than we normally recognize. So before selecting our "person" it is worth trying to picture who is likely to have been around. Second, we don't have to be the obvious person. Because we are female we don't have to choose a female participant etc. Because we are young we don't have to be a teenager. We don't have to play our "type-cast" character. Third, it is possible for us to "be" Jesus[1] – this is not necessarily arrogant, for through his Spirit we are supposed to be seeking for the mind of Christ! Finally, if I am preparing to lead a group I deliberately work through the passage being different characters. It is worth doing this a few times even if you are never going to lead a group. The process will show how varied are the insights any passage can bring; it is an enriching experience, but one which helps protect us from a tendency to reject other people's accounts as too fanciful!

3. Experience

Having ascertained *who* we are going to be, we then need to allow ourselves to enter fully into the passage. So, I pause again and ask God to control me, my imagination, and my experience. I like to affirm my trust in his sovereignty and his ability to speak to me through Scripture. I also indicate my desire to know him more fully, and my willingness to change and be changed.

Then I start to imagine what it was like to experience the event for the person I have chosen to be in the story. Initially the features of the story guide me, but I am also willing for my imagination to be led into something different. During this stage it helps if we ask ourselves as we enter into the context imaginatively what we are seeing, learning, feeling, touching, receiving, as well as what is going on, what is being said, and what actions are taking place. In order to help people get started on what is for many a very strange and difficult approach to Scripture I would say something like the following, in connection with the story of the paralytic, for instance.

I hope that by now you are beginning to enjoy yourselves and that you have associated yourself with someone in the scene. I now want you to try to become that person – you can walk into the TV screen and become a real-life person, so to speak. Try to allow your imagination to take control. In a way this is a kind of game, so let yourself go and don't try to stop yourself. Try to feel what it is like to be the person you have chosen to be. I think it might help us if I show you the kind of thing I mean. Let's suppose I am someone outside the house, an ordinary member of the crowd who can't get inside. Why am I outside, is it just because of the numbers or do I think I couldn't cope with the heat? Was I too late to be able to get in, or as the house filled up did I find I was getting squeezed out? Didn't I want to get too close to Jesus anyway?

Do I feel frustrated now, knowing Jesus is inside, or am I glad that I can hear him but that he cannot see me? Do I wish Jesus could see me? Do I hear everything he says or do I find it hard to hear him some of the time? What is he talking about? Do I sometimes pretend I haven't heard when the words he utters disturb me? How do I feel towards the crowd? Was it the crowd that attracted me and so I feel warm towards them, or am I angry that they keep me away from Jesus? Do these feelings tell me anything about my relationship with Jesus?

Do I think Jesus has talked long enough? Would I like to get away, but cannot, because of the crowd behind me? Am I afraid of what they might think if I walked away? Can I see Jesus through the door?

Then, I hear a commotion! I turn and see some men pushing through the crowd. I hear shouts and sense the waves of anger from the crowd who resent the intrusion. How do I react? Do I feel pushed by others, do I push back? Do I feel anger or do I try to calm others because I am afraid of angry feelings? Someone treads on my toe – do I give him a dirty look or dig him with my elbow? Then I see four people carrying a man who is sick. Do I feel guilty that I am in their way, or because I see he is my friend, or workmate, or fiancee, or child or wife – is there someone I want to bring to Jesus but am afraid to help? Or am I annoyed that the four thought of it beforehand and didn't ask me to help?

They carry him on to the roof. Do they stack the roofing neatly or throw it down? How do I react to them? Perhaps I am frightened by the unconventionality, perhaps I am annoyed that they interrupt Jesus, perhaps I am fearful lest they fall?

I see the paralytic let down to Jesus. Do I hope Jesus will be cross, or that the man will fall off his bed, or do I want him to be healed? Do I believe Jesus can do that or do I think they are fools to bother Jesus with impossibilities? Am I afraid that if he is healed I shall be challenged by who Jesus is?

After a long delay the man – the paralytic – comes out of the house carrying his bed. Am I amazed or angry – why should he get special treatment? What is he going to be like for a neighbour now? Was I able to look down on his weakness before?

I hope that from this illustration you will see how you can discover what happens to the person you identify with. Allow your imagination to free-wheel, the road is the framework of the story, but from time to time your imagination will need fresh impetus which you provide by asking questions. As you discover what happens to you I suggest that you make occasional notes of your reactions. I would encourage you to allow yourself to feel the emotions. Most of us have learnt from childhood that it is wrong to be angry or jealous or spiteful etc., but today let your feelings, in terms of the story, be acknowledged. This is important because they are part of us, even if normally they are buried in our subconscious. God knows about them anyway, and he still loves us, but he cannot begin to help us until we accept that they are there.

Christian Counsellors' Journal, vol. 2/4, pp. 8–9

I hope that this will help you, if you need the help. One thing I have found is that often nothing happens to me until I have given up – so please don't despair. Sometimes expectations and pressures we put upon ourselves act as a barrier and hinder the process. It really doesn't matter if we think we have got nowhere – God still loves us and values our willingness.

REVIEW

The final stage in the process is to review what we have experienced. In order to do this we need to interpret what our experience has been, something like decoding the Narnia Chronicles or even *Pilgrim's Progress*. There is no absolute way of knowing what is or is not significant, but at least we need to know the details of the imaginative journey we have taken. So a pre-requisite for our review is to have something to review. Some people will find it possible to come in and out of their experience. So, for instance, every few minutes they can write down what has happened "so far", then return to their experience. Others will find this too disruptive and will need to wait until the end, and then write down all they can recall. Again, even with the rather mechanical process of recording it is valid and important to seek God's help. He can be at work bringing the important features to our remembrance. It is not good to exclude aspects of our experience we think are not very important, for it may be just these that God will use during the review phase.

Having compiled a brief record of our experience it is time to invite God to speak to us through it. It may be that the experience has brought with it its own meaning; but this is not always so. Perhaps we sense something is significant, but we can't sort out what it means. Often just staying with the issue and saying to God "Please show me what this means" is enough – gradually God will present us with his truth and as he does so we have a dual responsibility.

On the one hand we need to check out that what we sense is the meaning is in tune with God's general revelation in Scripture. If it isn't then we need to put this on one side, or ask God to show us his truth. We are always prone to being misled, either from our own imaginations or from Satan's suggestions. As Jesus shows us by the way he handled his temptations, Scripture is the touchstone for truth, it is the light that will reveal the error and guide our paths.

Your word is a lamp to guide me and a light for my path.

Psalm 119.105

On the other hand, our second responsibility is to thank God for what he is showing us, even if it is uncomfortable, and to ask him to reveal more. This open-heartedness to God, this desire to "seek his face" is often a prerequisite for the whole process to work effectively.

How do we handle this if we are not sure? Suppose that the meaning is not clearly contrary to Scripture, but we are hesitant to affirm it as God's truth for us; what then? My recommendation is to tell God how we see the situation, but also to thank him that he is with us and working things through. We have asked the Holy Spirit to supervise the whole process and the more we are in touch with God the less happy Satan will be. So, even if there should be some kind of spiritual interference in the process, thanking God, and affirming our commitment to him will help us. It is one way of resisting the devil and we are promised that if we do he will flee (James 4.7).

My experience is that this review stage often becomes a dialogue with God. If this meditation is taking place in a group context, then there are some other approaches available. Often it is helpful for those for whom the process is new, or for those who find it difficult, to take them through the review a step at a time. Some people will really feel "I can't manage this; I'm no good at it", when all they need is some practical encouragement. The following steps may help (however, please assure people that no one has to share anything they don't want to – it is most important and proper to preserve people's freedoms).

1. Ask the group members to indicate which of several key characters they were. It is always worth asking who was someone completely different. It is also worth assuring people that it's fine to be whoever they were – often there is guilt and fear prevalent.

2. Ask the group if anyone wishes to share something they experienced. I have always found some who want to do this. Next we can ask whether they understand what God was saying to them through their experiences. If not we can invite others to comment. Again it is important to protect the person who has made themselves vulnerable by sharing. I always make it clear that "guilt-loading" interpretations are not from God, and any interpretation must be offered in a spirit of love; it must be an offer, not a categorical, authoritative, final word. Normally I would model features by comments I would make. It is helpful to set the style and the tone in this way. Questions such as "Why do you think that feature stuck in your mind?" or "Could it be that God is suggesting…?" Again I would interlace this process with appropriate short prayers and words of appreciation to those who have volunteered their imaginative

journey to the whole group. If no one seems to have a specific understanding of the shared account, then it is scripturally legitimate to ask God to give us some clarifying insight. However, there is no need to panic; just as Jesus frequently did not explain his parables to the crowds because living with the story was part of the process of revelation, so it may well be that God sometimes chooses to leave us with the uninterpreted experience. So, if there is no explanation forthcoming, encourage people to go on thanking God and telling him that his servants are listening expectantly. This is not letting us or God off the hook; it is trusting his sovereignty. As we shall soon see, we can actively co-operate in the process by reusing the experience. (The epilogue section explains how this can be done.) Once we have reviewed our imaginative journey and attempted to understand its significance within our own real life-frame, ensuring, of course, that such understanding is compatible with Scripture and the character of God, then it is time to consider the epilogue phase.

THE EPILOGUE

Probably this is a less than helpful term, because in many ways there need be no final end point to the process. Our imaginative journey does not have to end. God may go on using it. What I wish to convey through the word "epilogue" is that normally it is proper and helpful for us to handle aspects of our imaginative journey away from the main process. It is good to give thanks to God for what we have experienced – if nothing else we will have had a quiet half-hour! It is also useful to put down some markers for ourselves, very soon after the end of the biblical meditation. These markers may well include notes of issues to look at, noting a time in our diary when we will review what has happened, in the presence of God, or talk things over with a well-trusted Christian friend. Sensitized memories can easily be lost. Just as ripe fruit can soon become rotten, so in some way or other we do well to harvest our crop of experiences. Nevertheless, whether we have undertaken our experience in the privacy of our own homes, or in a group context directed by a leader, there may well be features of our discovery which need longer for us to assimilate properly. Sometimes we can sense God showing us issues which need a deeper privacy for us to become more sure what actions are

required on our part. On other occasions we may become aware
that there are hurts which need healing, or personal barriers, which
require God's help if they are to be removed. Such processes can
take a long time, certainly longer than the meditation time allows.

In such cases, one positive and creative way to carry out this
epilogue phase is deliberately to recall our story experience and
then to work through issues within the context of the story, by
imaginatively taking control of events. So, for instance, if we
return to the healing of the paralytic, someone might have
experienced a problem in removing the roof if, instead of being
tiles or branches and mud, which could easily be removed, the roof
turned out to be concrete. Perhaps this indicated a sense of
difficulty for them in getting through to God. Now, it might be that
this helped the person come to terms with a deliberate sin in their
lives. In which case, through repentance, confession and receiving
forgiveness from God, together with support to help them change
their life-style, all would be well. However, they may not know
what the problem is. So first they can give thanks to God – he
knows their problem and wants to sort it out for them. But, what
then? Perhaps when they are relaxed at home, even in bed, they can
ask God to help them. Then they re-enter the story. At first they
may choose to see if the roof is still concrete – perhaps they are
already changing, and this will be mirrored in the way they
experience the story.

If not, they can go mentally prepared! They can look for a skylight
with a ladder and get in that way. Maybe they will have the
wonderful surprise of finding Jesus waiting to help them down off
the ladder! Or maybe they can bring some workers with a pneumatic
drill to get through, or...? What I am suggesting is that we can work
through our "problem" within the framework of the story. I believe
this is legitimate because we know God wants us to seek for him and
has promised we will find him if we seek with all our hearts. I
believe it can be helpful because if we are prayerful about the whole
process then God will be influencing the strategy we choose to break
through the roof, and will use this to help us discover and overcome
the barriers. He may even use it to get rid of the barriers without us
ever knowing what they were. The results will not be limited to the
story level; if God has worked it will impact our lives and there will
be a new quality in our relationship with God.

Obviously the details are going to vary according to the
scriptural material which was the framework for our journey, the
details of our personal experience within that journey, and

the issues which are being focused through it. It is the legitimacy of the approach and how to operate it which I am presenting. Again, however, please note that it is not legitimate to make anything happen – only things which we know from Scripture are according to God's will. In no way is this approach to be considered a mechanism for manipulating God, or even for convincing ourselves (falsely) that we can do so. Rather, it is a way of surrendering our imaginations to God, a means of presenting this part of our whole selves to him as a living sacrifice.

I am sure that there are other ways of involving this aspect of our personalities. Others would emphasize the value of our dreams for instance. Others may find writing stories another way in which God shares himself with them. Although I prefer my method and I think I do so because it is rooted in Scripture, I do not wish to minimize God's creativity. All I would plead for is that in some way, particularly by bathing the whole process in prayer, checking "insights" against Scripture, sharing "truths" with Christian friends and noting the results, the fruit, against Christian standards – we ensure that we are not carried away by our own vain imaginings!

Suggested Activities

1. How would you distinguish fantasy and imagination?

2. Consider "the truths" that are conveyed through some of the television cartoons. Are these "truths" ones which are consistent with the Christian faith?

3. Work through an imaginative Bible study – some other passages you might like to try are Matthew 9.18–25; 12.9–12; 21.1–11; 26.26–30.

Notes

1   If he is in the situation – the same goes for any other leading character – we could be the angel or the emperor!

7 LOOKING AROUND

We have now collected ourselves together, ready for our exploration of God in our world. We have noted that because this is God's world he can meet with us through it because it reflects his personhood to some extent, but also, because he is master of it he can use it to communicate more directly. Further, because people are made in his image, this includes a parallel but derivative creative ability. So, it is not only the natural world but the manufactured and created "world of man" which has the potential as a meeting point with God. There are also valid reasons for recognizing that the process as well as the results have this kind of potential. The Scriptures bear witness to the fact that this is not only theoretically true but is validated in practice by the way God operates and the situations in which people meet God.

We recognize too that there is potential for awareness within ourselves which we often ignore or eliminate. We have made a small start in becoming aware of our greater potential to receive input from our environment. However, through our environment we may also receive signals from God. The reason for this, in a simplified way, is well expressed by Hanchey:

> But if God is so close to us, why don't we sense God's care any more than we do? Here's one reason why. Human consciousness can be pictured as an iceberg. We see only simple consciousness, what we know and what we're consciously aware of. Just under the surface is semi-consciousness, or what we suspect and sense, and deeper still there resides our subconsciousness mind, what we don't consciously know, but of which we are deeply aware, nevertheless. Of course, these distinctions are artificial, but they serve to describe the complexity of our mental processes and the deeply pervasive way God is with us...
>
> At deep human levels there is a lot more communion between God and us than most Christian theology imagines. [1]

It is time for us now to start our journey of exploration. Just as we discovered that if we look more quietly, listen more alertly, and touch more patiently we can discover more going on around us or even within us than we realized, so our journey through the next few chapters should help us discover God is wanting to say more to us than we realized. Of course, it is possible that when we stop to listen there really are no sounds to hear, and it is possible that God is not saying anything. Don't be too discouraged by this possibility – it is most unlikely. Much more likely is the following radio "metaphor":

> *Take your portable radio and listen – nothing! Why? Because it needs to be switched on. Switch it on – there might still be nothing for several reasons. The batteries are drained of power, or it is a mains/battery powered one and you are switched on to the wrong source. Maybe you are in between frequencies, or the radio has broken, or you have suddenly and unexpectedly gone deaf. Perhaps the radio station to which you are tuned has gone off the air. Most of these possibilities are unlikely and most can be checked out fairly quickly.*

For example:

- *No power – try some new batteries – check mains/battery switch is in the right position*

- *In between – turn tuning knob or press frequencies button (as appropriate)*

- *Radio station dead – turn to another frequency*

- *Gone deaf – listen for other sounds or ask someone else to listen to your radio*

- *Radio broken – try another radio!*

Because it is highly unlikely that there are no messages being transmitted at all on any frequency we normally explore all the other options first before coming to this conclusion. I believe we should think the same way about God. The world in which we live is busy with his messages and there are some very personal ones he wants to get through to us. When this happens to us for the first time it can be perplexing and startling. So be encouraged – there are many reasons why at first you may not hear much from God, the two least likely are that God isn't saying anything to anyone let alone you, and second that you are completely incapable of hearing anything from him.[2] I sometimes struggle with electrical equipment, especially when it is new (I can never totally follow the written instructions). If the kind of meditation we are embarking on is new to you, or if indeed the whole idea of meditation seems strange, then please understand it is rather like working with a new radio. If it helps you to persevere with the process which follows in this book then remember the parallel. It may help you to "handle yourself" by comparing how you respond in the sort of "equipment situation" I have described. Some of us are frightened we have broken the new equipment and we panic! Some people, however, are more adventurous – they will twiddle with knobs and push buttons until something happens. Some people read the instruction booklet meticulously – it may work that way; but often I find something has been altered or something vital remains unexplained in the instructions, which throws everything out. Anyway if we only read the booklet we'll never hear the radio – there has to be "hands-on" experience sooner or later. Some people will take the radio to someone else to show them how it works. How do you react? It may give you clues about your reactions to meditation and hopefully help you to overcome initial barriers.

Are your responses to "meditation" similar or different? If you do get stuck or seem to be getting nowhere, think through how you would handle the situation if it were "the radio" and apply the solution in the "meditation" context.

What follows are a few ideas. Remember two very important things about your freedom.

1. Please don't expect that as you "look around" in the directions that I indicate you will necessarily see the same things or "hear" the same things from God as I did. My accounts are meant to start the process but you should follow through your own perceptions.

2. You may soon find yourself looking at other things and situations entirely – that's great. Please don't be restricted to situations and responses to which I may point. The process is like learning a new language – the words and phrases I suggest are so you can speak, build fluency and confidence, so you can say what you wish to say and hear what others are saying to you.

Look in the gutter. The other day I was strolling along and I spent a few moments just looking in the gutter. (Perhaps I choose this as a starting point because of other things I have learnt through

observing the rubbish!) This exercise is not easy to do if the street
is in a shopping centre – although perhaps you can do it if you are
waiting for a bus. There was a Coke can, some scraps of paper, and
a few other things. It was the Coke can that gained my attention. It
is very much a sign of modernity with all the hyped-up advertising,
the careful design there had been, all the technical skills to
manufacture such a light metal object, and so on. I realized that it
had been purchased by someone and had been used by them to
quench their thirst as they had drunk its contents, and then it had
been discarded. Probably a car had run over it and squashed it,
although perhaps some teenager had crushed it in their hand before
throwing it down. In any case it was now distorted out of shape
completely. Thrown down, or squidging out from under a wheel it
had eventually found some kind of temporary resting place lodged
in the gutter. In a few days either a strong gust of wind would send
it rolling reluctantly further down the street or more likely the road
sweeping machine would suck it up and send it, along with
multitudinous refuse, to the incinerator.

Reflecting on this observation afterwards, I realized there were
many directions in which my thinking could have moved. I could
have been angry that some person uncaring about the environment
had not only cluttered the gutter, giving a sense of untidiness and
lack of care, but had also added an extra risk, for if someone should
fall they could cut themselves on the now exposed edge of the can...
and so I might have reflected about the way sin works; a thoughtless
act spoils the environment, processed by someone else's unavoidable
response (the car crushing it) it now becomes dangerous as well as
disagreeable, yet it was within my power to restore – I could have
taken the can home with me. I could also have thought about the way
social conditions contribute to the problem – there are no litter bins
in the street! I could have concentrated on the way a now ugly object
had been the vehicle of refreshment on a hot summer's day, of the
contrast between the content and the container. My mind could have
focused on the way technology tends to irresponsibility, for the Coke
manufacturer's major concern was with selling the product. Clearly
great care goes into promotion, distribution, economy, and attractiveness of the container, even the cunning design, but maybe not enough
attention is given to "what happens afterwards". When the product is
sold it becomes "their responsibility". Multiply this attitude and we
have the vast environmental problems which threaten to destroy
God's world. But it was, in fact, none of these tracks I actually
went down.

Rather, I saw in the crumpled, crushed, derelict can a deeply felt challenge to remember the care and competence that had gone into its manufacture and design. I felt not anger but sadness that so much investment was now distorted and disregarded by all but, for the moment, me. I realized that when God looks on an old person no longer able to go out – widowed perhaps, living alone, their potential all but spent – limbs barely able to carry the misformed body, youth no longer even conceivable, vigour vacated, hopes run dry, then, he remembers their beauty, their courage, and the life he gave them and why.

That old, crumpled can became a powerful challenge to respect not only them but also a stimulus to rekindle within me the awareness of the value of each person I met, not only those who might think they have passed their sell-by date but those, too, whose form (not only physical, but mental and moral and spiritual) was now disformed. For their present perceivable state was not the truth about them. It was not for "this" they were created, but for a great glory – each part carefully considered and made for a wholesome purpose. And if my observation of a derelict Coke can could, in a few moments of time, create or draw out such values, with what could God's eternal awareness of each person's existence, endow them. No longer could I see an object in the gutter but rather a challenge to care for people and place them in God's perspectives.

There were many other tatters that lay there too, such as a cigarette stub, a few leaves, scraps of paper, the signs of primitive life forming on the tarmac surface – each could have spoken to me of God's truth. What will you see?

Each day I'm at home I eat my breakfast sitting on a stool, at our breakfast bar looking at our neighbour's dwelling! I see familiar scenes – bricks, windows, drainpipes, nothing very unusual, a rolled hosepipe attached to an outside tap waiting to water the tomatoes growing in the greenhouse or shower the car. However, for a few weeks an additional object focused my sight. It was a panel of fencing. It was ordinary fencing. At first I wondered why it stood waiting – was it superfluous to the number required? But then I began to see other things. First I could see some circular marks on it. I realized I was looking at the evidence of how each strip of timber had been cut. Instinctively my mind went back to a visit I had made with several other theological students to the British Rail carriage works at Derby. In particular I heard again the scream, intense, awesome noise of very powerful saws cutting through thick timber.

The shriek of the saw was like a cry of pain. Even at that time I realized that this was fantasy but the memory has always lingered with me. Because of these memories the configuration on the sole, silent panel, those rough circular grooves, told me a tale of a painful process. I heard God say to me "Look carefully for the signs of pain in people. Look carefully at other people – do not rush by them – they may not shout or demand attention but hidden within them is pain I see – learn to see it too".

Then the Lord said, "I have seen how cruelly my people are being treated in Egypt".

Exodus 3.7

All may look orderly, peaceful, and in control, but one small scar may remain. It is not always a physical scar, of course. It may be a slightly more intense reaction to a comment than would be normal; it may be a shift in the eyes, it may be a tendency to withdraw, a hesitation to accept responsibility, a reluctance to shake hands which is there even when normal courtesies are being observed – "learn to see the marks of painful process" God was saying to me. Only because I saw the panel for several days and had nothing better to do, was I able to notice. Only because of a previous experience was I able to explain and "understand" for myself the significance of those marks, which many would never notice even if they saw them, because they could not give them a meaning. So, God was saying to me that I might not even notice the tell-tale marks, and even when I did I would not truly see. "Look with a gentle, quiet, loving respect towards those you see regularly but may not know too well – there will be much to discover. Don't criticize others, learn to understand their reactions and responses as indicators of their painful history and do not dismiss them, because in your eyes they are imperfect." God knows all the processes each of us have been through and he "sees" the traces in my life and he understands. This is why Christ's experience of human life is so important to the Godhead and to us. This is clearly and beautifully expressed in a New Testament passage:

We have a great High Priest who has gone into the very presence of God – Jesus the Son of God. Our High Priest is not one who cannot feel sympathy for our weaknesses. On the contrary, we have a High Priest who was tempted in every way that we are, but did not sin.

Hebrews 4.14–16

So I know that I can rest before the awesome God and realize he understands me. I can even ask God to show me the "marks" in my life and to help me understand he appreciates me even more because of the blemishes, imperfections, and scars which I hide from others, and even become unaware of myself.

There was a second observation which led me Godwards as I looked at that cheap fencing panel. In the strips of timber were several "knots". My first reaction as I looked at them was to get angry about them. Why? Well I know that they are likely to dry out, shrink and fall out leaving holes and areas of weakness in the fencing. It was a pity that they were there. In some timbers, properly sanded and polished, such deformities would add greatly to the interest and intricacy of the wood and could give a quiet pleasure to a thousand eyes which would be soothed by the flowing lines, without ever realizing the original purpose of the visual symphony that was bathing their psyches. But in such functional timber they were a nuisance and that was that. Then God said "David, hold on a minute". "What Lord?" "Tell me what those knots indicate." "Well, Lord, that is where the branches of the fir tree grew out from the main stream." "Yes, David – so what would happen to the trunk if there had been no knots and hence no branches?" "There would have been no trunk, no timber, no fence." So it is that often the "blemishes", the "imperfections", the weaknesses have made the useful, the strong, the desirable, possible at all.

It is sometimes true within a family where the weaker members have actually contributed so much to the strong. It is often true within a group that those who appear to be "passengers" are the ones that service the group, and keep it together and able to function cohesively. It may well be the case in my life; those experiences I wish were not there because they seem like potential weak points in my memories – those character traits which I despise in myself, may well be the source of strength, determination, patience, humour, openness, and generosity without which I wouldn't be me.

This small and temporary trouble we suffer will bring us an... eternal glory, much greater than the trouble.

2 Corinthians 4.17

How important it was for me to move beyond the disfigurements in the wood to consider what they represented and the functions they fulfilled.

For we fix our attention, not on things that are seen, but on things that are unseen.

2 Corinthians 4.18

Inevitably a further reality hit me between the eyes. How selfishly we view things. I felt anger about the knots because I was thinking of the purpose for which the panel of fencing was made. I did not think of the tree and its needs to grow. I did not think of the pleasure and protection that those outstretched branches had given to thousands of human beings who had seen the tree flourishing on some hillside, and the thousands of birds and animals who had benefited from the shelter it gave. As I realized how selfish I had been in my response to the knots, a question pressed in on me. "How can we avoid claiming the right to evaluate everything from its value to me?" My perspective was dominating the whole valuation of the object, and it is not a huge leap from this position to evaluating every human being, as well as everything else, from the same selfish standpoint.

How cuttingly the image of Christ the servant from Paul's letter to the Philippians, struck home. The prelude goes like this:

Don't do anything from selfish ambition,... be humble towards one another, always considering others better than yourselves. And look out for one another's interests, not just for your own. The attitude you should have is the one that Christ Jesus had.

Philippians 2.3–5

These first two subjects for meditation and reflection have been static ones. But if our modern world is anything, it is moving, rush, frantic activity, busyness and mobility. Science has revealed to us an amazingly mobile and volatile world. The solid table on which I rest my paper to write is made up of atoms, and each atom has whirling electrons. From the sub-microscopic to the supra mega the story is the same. For the whole universe is moving at ever increasing speeds away from its centre of origin. So, any book which deals with meditation in the modern world must deal with hectic activity too.

One of the places to go to see such "rush" is a bridge over a motorway. On a good day it will be a picture of endless motion – on a bad day the traffic will be stationary! Today is a good day. What, I wonder, would an "unsuspecting visitor from Mars" make of it? In one direction, cars of many colours and shapes, lorries with harsh contours, coaches, sleek but also sometimes blunt, daring motorcycles all flow away from under our feet, all moving, steering along, interweaving, interacting, obeying some strange laws. In the other direction, with menacing ferocity a similar mix charges towards us. It seems as though forever the traffic discharges itself in both directions down the six or eight lanes like blood cells in arteries and veins. The traffic flow can appear to be some weird mechanistic process, impersonal and deterministic. Yet the reality is that each vehicle is driven with a purpose. Many cars have passengers who share a common life, a family talking, listening, playing, responding, encouraging. Each person has their own thoughts, perceptions of the journey, feelings, yet corporately going together somewhere – on a shopping spree, a holiday, to visit grandma – whatever it may be. Within each body a detailed, delicate, and programmed process is taking place. Each lorry driver has his or her own personal agenda, but each has a destination to which the cargo must be delivered – a factory waiting for its parts so that the production line can continue, a distribution depot waiting for its contents so they can be dispersed to retail outlets and numerous customers satisfied (we hope). Each coach, a microcosm; a basketful of nationalities and personality types and varied ultimate destinations but for a few brief hours, involuntarily sharing the same air and destiny.

Standing on the bridge, with my brain bombarded with the pounding of the traffic noise there is just about space to think such thoughts! The challenge here revolves around the clash of perceptions. Which is the right interpretation of the phenomenon before my eyes? My eyes and ears tell me of a mechanistic, deterministic impersonal process – the rush of machines – a flow which can be measured and predicted. My understanding contradicts this because I realize each individual unit is driven with a personal purpose and is not, as at first appears, a mindless rush towards extinction. Which is the right interpretation of the universe?

The personal explanations seem to me more true, more fundamental, more valid, more real. It is only when we generalize, by distancing ourselves from the individual situation, that the impersonal takes over and seems to gain credibility. But how can we cope with speed, numbers, and noise without voiding our experiences of personal truth? Without the personal truth we don't even drive properly. It is because we start to forget that there is a real person who has needs, weaknesses etc. in every other car, that we drive with less courtesy and consideration than we would normally do. Hanging on to the personal dimension of the statistical and numerical side of life is a very important challenge. Yet living with such an awareness for everyone of the tens of thousands of vehicles that thunder under the motorway bridge is an exhausting task, which leaves us without the energy and sensitivity to deal generously and creatively with the truly personal situations that are ours.

Is this an area where I need God's help? I sense it is, for Scripture shows us a God who can cope with enormous numbers in a personal way: sparrows in the street and hairs on a head are nothing to him.

> *To whom can the Holy God be compared?*
> *Look up at the sky!*
> *Who created the stars you see?*
> *The one who leads them out like an army,*
> *he knows how many there are*
> *and calls each one by name!*
> *His power is so great.*

Isaiah 40.25–26

He strengthens those who are weak and tired. Those who trust in the Lord for help will find their strength renewed.

Isaiah 40.29, 31

Come to me, all of you who are tired from carrying heavy loads, and I will give you rest. Take my yoke and put it on you, and learn from me…

Matthew 11.28–29

With each of these meditations there are many routes we may travel down, many roads we may hear God calling us to travel to find his Word to us, many rooms we may enter into and find his message. It is not for me to direct you; my purpose in writing is mainly to say "This can be God's call too", "He is to be found there also". However, if it helps, here are a few more leads, particularly for the motorway meditation.

As the traffic moves under your feet, maybe a particular vehicle catches your eye – perhaps it is a foreign lorry. Why not discover more about the country, find out what sort of things they export, what the conditions of those who manufacture them are like, where the goods might be going. Try to appreciate what the driver feels like, so far away from home etc.

You may find your attention absorbed by the social and economic environmental issues which such movement of population involves.

You could also consider the contrast between the static road and the speed of the traffic. In order for such facility of human interactivity something needs to be constant, dependable, reliable. Are there people and situations for which you need to be the road? Are there people who have been or who are the motorway over which you travel? Is there some aspect of your life which needs to be kept in good repair to give you the stability you need in order to live the rest of your life at a hectic speed. What happens if you neglect the roadway? Is this one reason why God is so necessary for us in our world?

Here, then, are a few more avenues to explore the motorway theme for meditation. But we too must now move on.

Notes

1   Hanchey, *Church Growth and the Power of Evangelism* (Cowley Publications, Cambridge Massachusetts, 1990).

2   Incidentally the parallel I have drawn about the radio is itself an applied accidental meditation – or series of meditations.

8 LOOKING INWARDS

Vehicles on the move were the focus for the last meditation in Chapter 7. We stay with them as we move towards a different dimension of meditation which would often be called "the journey inwards". Few people can remain unmoved by the marvel and surprise of seeing the detailed, intricate, delicate structure of a snowflake. Somehow the discovery of such beauty within common materials opens us up to an awareness that there may be other wonders hidden, ignored, passed over within our world. J. John, the English Evangelist, recounts how he was extolling the wonder of snowflakes and explaining that it is said "no two snowflakes are alike". He added that he wondered who it was who had the job of examining them all. After his meeting a man approached him and said he had spent the last seventeen years of his life looking at snowflakes! Again the unexpected – the speaker never knows who is in his audience and what surprises they may bring!

In different ways, as we journey inwards, into the products of our modern technology, there may be as many discoveries and glimpses of God as in the examination and observation of the internal structure of a flower, or a cell, or a molecule like DNA. Such hints of God are not normally the result of observation alone, rather they are the product of such observation interacting with, maybe even clashing with, our normal perception of the objects. It is the sense of surprise, of a hidden order within, which calls us to move beyond to the hidden depths where traces of God's passing through greet us. I believe it can be the same with human ingenuity, although we need, maybe, to develop a greater awareness of humankind being made in God's image. This will need to direct us beyond the human to the image, i.e. to the true but inadequate representation of God.

Where should we begin? My suggestion is that we start with a visit to the car. Not to leap into it with a rush to the station to catch a train, or to the supermarket to cram a trolley with "necessities", nor even to the garage to fill up with petrol. Rather that we "stand and stare" at what makes it all happen. We go to the bonnet, recall where the catch is and (if you are at all like me) eventually manage to lift the lid. What then? Well, here at least is my journey.

I am confronted with a cacophony of shapes. I use the word cacophony metaphorically, of course, but it is used deliberately. All those strange shapes – metal, plastic or what have you, apparently thrown together at random angles and levels, linked together with tubes and wire – all of this creates in my head the same panic-filled reaction as a sounding gong or clashing cymbals. I am baffled, confused, overwhelmed, indeed daunted by what I know is meant to make sense, as well as make the car go. I know it is not random but planned and precision built. But to all intents it looks to me as chaotic as the groceries in a shopping trolley.

Over the years I have been forced to look more carefully and constructively at the objects under the bonnet, indeed bonnets. I have learnt that some things are arbitrary. One model will have the spare wheel stored here, another the jack. Sometimes a necessary object which is fairly easily identifiable even to the novice like myself, e.g. the battery, will not be under the bonnet, but hidden in the boot. I soon learnt to identify where fluids had to be tipped – the water or anti-freeze, the oil, although the dip-stick to measure it occupied a different orifice, the wash-bottle for the windscreen, the brake fluid reservoir and so on. Then there is the engine block itself – I have never ventured further into the mysteries of this power source than the plugs – although visits to the local garage have convinced me that it must be a miniature version of a black hole, for how all these internal workings can fit into such a small container is beyond my wildest imaginations. But gradually, as I make myself overcome the initial panic, a few other parts become recognizable – the distributor, the alternator, the starting motor, the radiator, the fan and that's about my limit.

A car engine is such a strange mixture of shapes large and small, erratic and regular; of materials, steel, aluminium, plastic, solid and flexible; of regimes mechanical and electrical; of motion fixed, flexible, and meant to move. But how can all of this help me to find God?

First it speaks to me of purpose in apparent chaos. Every part, and the position of every part in relationship to every other part, is planned. It is primarily planned to move the car as efficiently as possible, but it is also planned to integrate with the space available, with safety factors taken into account and an occasional thought is spared for the mechanic who will need to service the engine (although my own experience in this field of

activity, severely limited as it certainly is, suggests that everything has been planned to make the amateur's task as difficult,
painful, and frustrating as possible – when you drop a nut it
doesn't even fall on to the floor but finds a ledge on which to
hold itself). So the apparent chaos of the car engine is a call to
me to look again at the apparently disconnected, irregular,
unpredictable anomalous blocks of life – my life and other
people's, and to stand quietly and look carefully – not to rush
into a mental panic but try to see if I can recognize anything
familiar in the bewildering and then to begin to plot my way
through the unusual. "Could it be that this is that?" "Does that
connection give me a clue as to why the other?" and so on.

I realize that two things have helped me glean a little awareness of a car engine. The first is the guidance of others, such as
my father who came to my rescue when our first car turned to
steam – one of the hoses had ruptured. He began to explain the
parts and the purposes. From then on a number of friends and
even garage mechanics have tried to help me grasp the mystery.
The second is the car handbook which is not always the most
helpful guide that I can imagine! So often it seems to be telling
me what I already know, or what I don't need to know, but only
rarely explaining with sufficient clarity and detail the things I
really need to know at the time. But those rare occasions make
the guide invaluable, and, if I am really honest, it is quite a
comfort to have confirmed the things I think I already know.
Similarly, two things help me grasp the mystery of "life's part".
The insight and guidance of some friends – often given at a time
of crisis, but not always, and God's guidebook, the Bible, not
always explaining issues in the order that I would select, often
leaving me groping when I long for detail and precision – yet
enough to help me through the maze.

Your time with a car engine may have quite different results
for you. Perhaps you are a competent engineer – you can admire
the precision engineering and the advancing technology or you
can look at it and feel very much at home – knowing your way
round it as you do your own home, at ease with it, knowing you
have mastered its failings many times before. For someone else it
will be a dirty, unnecessary mess, that you would rather never
look at and you cannot imagine how anyone could think such an
ugly monstrosity could ever speak of God.

Whichever your response, please spend time with the engine;
look at it, listen to your own reactions, and try and understand

them, surrender them and invite God to speak to you through it all. Look quietly, look from different angles, look with amazement and see what you begin to hear from the Almighty who gave to humankind such ingenuity. And how was it that he knew so many millions of years ago that in the nineteenth and twentieth centuries, at a particular time in the developing complexity of human life, we should need vast underground lakes of oil to provide us with the flexible mobility of the car to cope with urbanization and relationships? Or, is the car the creator of unbridled pollution that threatens to deplete the oil and choke the inhabitants of the world, the arch-symbol of people's greed and depersonalization?

Looking at a car engine can be a cold business in winter, so for our next opportunity for discovery, let's come back indoors. A car engine is also large and unmanageable. Some of us find it easier when we can hold things in our hands, so our next object of meditation is a common household electrical plug. Many of us don't have a car, so we have had to count on the goodwill of friends for the last meditation as well as for our transport. Most of us will have several dozen plugs around the place – kettles, electrical fires, washing machines, fridge, video, iron, table lamps, hairdryers, CD players, televisions, keyboards, computers, typewriters, lawnmowers, electric blankets and power drills. And so we could extend the list. Unless you know what you are doing, I suggest you take a plug that is not in use, but preferably one that is "wired up".

Take the plug in your hand and have a good look at it. Is it a case of "familiarity breeds contempt"? Or is it something you already know, understand, and appreciate? Perhaps it will help to ask yourself why it is the shape it is and why it is made from the materials it is. It may be good to wait quietly for God to speak through this object as we look at it from the outside.

Perhaps he will speak to us about service or maybe power, or perhaps about home and country – for, of course, when you travel abroad there will almost certainly be a different design for the common domestic plug which will render all your electrical equipment useless. Perhaps it will be along entirely different lines that God will begin to speak through a plug.

For the next stage in this meditation we need, not matches to light the candle, but a screwdriver to undo the holding screw so that we can look inside the plug. Be careful as you take this screw out – some are fixed, but others seem programmed to drop

out and roll away. You will need this screw again so place it
carefully. Then you will discover two halves, one with almost
nothing about it, the other the one to which all the wires and
everything else are attached. Again this everyday object, so
cheaply available, is the product of enormous ingenuity and care.
Many will be familiar with the layout and will understand the
arrangement, but for those who are not the diagram below might
help you to find your way around.

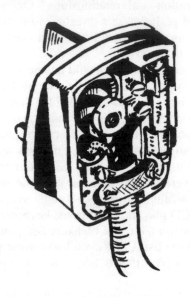

But now a warning – not about a health hazard – but about the fact
that there are so many ways in which the details can vary. Some
features remain constant but others, to do with style, ingenuity, cost
etc., may differ. So, I apologize if this diagram doesn't quite fit your
plug. Again you may want to pause and let God speak to you about
this very issue. What other realms share this same kind of mixture
of the standard and the idiosyncratic? How useful is it to have a
diagram, whether visual or mental? Do we use it to help us understand situations and people – or do we use it to avoid care with the
differentiating features that make situations and people distinct?

Have you ever tried "wiring a plug"? If you are in a group
sharing this exercise, may I suggest you turn to a neighbour and
talk about some of your experiences in this task. Have you ever
tried to teach someone how to wire a plug? What was your

experience here? How many factors and features which you take for granted then had to be thought through and explained?

What do you think about the way the plug you are holding has been wired? Is it safe, is it neat, is it sloppy and rushed or has it been worked out carefully with each wire cut to its distinct length according to its position in the plug? Did the person fitting the wire ever think their work would be examined so carefully? Would it have made any difference to the way they did the job? Does this say anything to us about our life and God and judgement?

Have you ever been the detective trying to discover why the light or the television won't work? Do you remember checking through the various features of the plug to see which, if any, was at fault – examining the neutral and the live cable to see that the screws are tight and in good contact with the bare wires, ensuring that the wires can't be pulled out and, naturally, checking the earth wire at the same time, wondering if the fuse was still OK. Which way did you work to solve the problem? Did you insert a new fuse in the suspect plug or test the fuse in another plug – say the one attached to a table lamp? Do you enjoy such challenges or find them annoying? We can stay with such experiences and see if God will speak through them. This can happen not only as we live them but as we relive them by using our memories.

Now take the whole plug to pieces, wires out, screws out, fuse out, retaining clamp out. Place all the bits and bobs in front of you. Isn't it amazing – how many individual parts go into one simple object – a few of them can be safely interchanged, the screws clamping the wires to the contacts for instance – but not many. Will God speak to you through the dismembered parts? One of the sets of things he says to me is similar to the insights Paul gives us about the Church as the body of Christ.

> *For the body itself is not made up of only one part, but of many parts. If the foot were to say, "Because I am not a hand, I don't belong to the body," that would not keep it from being a part of the body. And if the ear were to say, "Because I am not an eye, I don't belong to the body," that would not keep it from being a part of the body. If the whole body were just an eye, how could it hear? And if it were only an ear, how could it smell? As it is, however, God put every different part in the body just as*

he wanted it to be. There would not be a body if it were all only one part! As it is, there are many parts but one body.

So then, the eye cannot say to the hand, "I don't need you!" Nor can the head say to the feet, "Well, I don't need you!" On the contrary, we cannot do without the parts of the body that seem to be weaker; and those parts that we think aren't worth very much are the ones which we treat with greater care; while the parts of the body which don't look very nice are treated with special modesty, which the more beautiful parts do not need. God himself has put the body together in such a way as to give greater honour to those parts that need it. And so there is no division in the body, but all its different parts have the same concern for one another.

1 Corinthians 12.14–26

But in addition to all the points about the different parts, the varied functions, the mutual valuation, the interdependence etc. is now added the fact that I may dismember the body of Christ, as I have this plug!

Perhaps God will say completely different things to you. Again, if you are in a group context give yourselves ten minutes for reflections on this experience, five minutes to write them down, and then time to share your insights, grounding them in Scripture whenever possible. If you are on your own, why not write down your own encounter with the electric plug and share it with a friend or offer it to the editor of your church magazine.

So, we have dissected the plug and now it's time to reassemble it. Take your time, and try and capture your various feelings and thoughts as you do this. (Unless you are electrically competent, do get someone who is to check everything is correct before you think about using the plug again!) When everything is "back to normal", do you have a sense of satisfaction and achievement, or of anxiety and self-doubt about your competence – do you have a nagging feeling that something may not be right and the consequences could be serious? Can God say anything to you about yourself, your relationships or your attitudes, through this?

Suggested Activities

1. If you don't have a car available look at the inner workings of a television or a computer. (Please only do this if there is someone around who is competent to handle the electrics and explain the electronics!)

2. Instead of looking at the plug you hold in your hand, you could wander round your house with a similar sense of growing amazement as you think about the design, the functions for each part, the similarities and distinctiveness of your home compared with others. It is also worthy of note how each personality contributes to the overall effect! If people leave their mark, shouldn't we expect God so to do?

9 LOOKING BACKWARDS

Although Lot and his family were warned not to look backwards to the City of Sodom, this is unusual for the Bible. Constantly the Bible challenges us to remember, both in the Old and the New Testament:

Moses said to the people, "Remember this day – the day on which you left Egypt".

Exodus 13.3

Observe [remember] the Sabbath and keep it holy.

Exodus 20.8

Remember that you were slaves in Egypt, and that I, the Lord your God, rescued you by my great power and strength. That is why I command you to observe the Sabbath.

Deuteronomy 5.15

Remember how the Lord your God led you on this long journey through the desert these past forty years.

Deuteronomy 8.2

So remember your Creator while you are still young.

Ecclesiastes 12.1

Remember Lot's wife!

Luke 17.32

This is my body, which is for you. Do this in memory of me.

1 Corinthians 11.24

Remember your former leaders, who spoke God's message to you. Think back on how they lived and died, and imitate their faith.

Hebrews 13.7

Remembrance is an interactive process. Through it significance and perspective are given to contemporary happenings. This enables the participant to understand more accurately what is going on around them and, also, to know how to behave and live appropriately in their own context. Equally the past is enlivened by the sense of immediacy and relevance. The Bible knows little of a two-dimensional experience – the here and now. For believers there is a past (and future) dimension as well which generates a sense of identity and adds quality to the temporal experiences.

Scripture recognizes too that objects can be important for releasing the power of the past into the person's present. Thus stones were set up at Gilgal, and bread and wine are used "to remember" Jesus (Joshua 4; Luke 22). So, objects have amazing powers. They can operate like windows, so that with our "back to the future" we are allowed to look out on our own past and recapture many glimpses, separated in time and quality of experience – some will be trivial, others profound, one will be humorous, this one mundane, another painful, yet linked by the object on which our attention is focused. Or to put it another way, objects are like a day travel ticket – they allow us to travel down a time tube and revisit many previous experiences, to stop for as long or as short a time as we choose, to travel in an orderly or random way because the cost is already covered and factors other than economy may control our journey.

I have selected three common objects with this potential for me. My three may completely fail for you, so choose your own. If you can't choose because you are completely unused to this kind of encounter, then try objects from different realms – useful and artistic, visual or tactile. Or choose objects from different aspects of your life – family or work, home or leisure. Eventually, I think the process will begin to ignite for you.

But before I introduce you to my "objects" here are some preparatory reflections.

The day before I wrote this was the day after Christmas, it was also Sunday. So, on the television was a special young people's edition of the *Antiques Road Show*, held in the Science Museum, South Kensington, London. All kinds of objects were reviewed – stamps, jigsaws, fishing reels, dolls, powder compacts – partly they have value because of their rarity alone, partly because they represent special interests, partly because they are pictures from the book of social history. Yet, as well as a place in the history of manufacture and twentieth-century consumerism, each of them has a personal history. If only we could know who gave the doll to whom and how the doll was used – what joyful days the doll shared with some carefree child – and what happened as the years went by to child and doll. If only we could replay the fishing reel like a video tape and share the quiet deep pool of thoughts that passed through the mind of the person whose hands controlled the fishing tackle. If only we could see and understand the letter to which that earliest of Chinese stamps was attached – and if we could know how it came to be in the UK in the possession of a surprised young man. If only... but when it comes to us... did we have things which would now be of value?

One of the delights and, simultaneously, annoyances of that programme was that many of the objects which now have considerable and growing value are ones we have seen and handled and have thrown away. Not all, of course. Some are very special but many have come our way and because we did not glimpse their coming prestige, we have let them slip through our fingers. If only we had kept that box of old cigarette cards we played with as boys on our visit to grandma's! The same is almost true of our memories.

The other day I came across the following evocative account of memory:

> *Memory is the best of all gardens.*
> *Therein, winter and summer, the*
> *seeds of the past lie dormant, ready*
> *to spring into instant bloom at any moment*
> *the mind wishes to bring them to life.* [1]

But mostly we do not recognize their importance – at least not when they are being created. So many of them appeared ordinary, mundane, routine, insignificant moments – we did not know that they could be of any consequence. We surrender them to the knock of a playmate, the demand of an arriving bus, the call of a child needing help, the heartbeat of a waiting friend – by the time we could return to reclaim them, the uncertain wind of time had blown them away like autumn leaves and we did not even remember they had been there once.

"Almost true" but not quite – one of the strange powers of objects is that they can stir our memories, as though we can somehow play the film backwards and all that the wind has scattered returns to its starting point. So I hope that you will enter the reverse time zone as memories are released by looking backwards. There will be many wonderful moments you relive which will deeply enhance your sense of the quality of your life. I hope that through this very process you will sense the blessing of God on and in your life, and that within you there will be your own "Hallelujah Chorus". Yet, I am aware that buried with us there can be more difficult memories which will be released like an animal freed from a cage, raging about, doing damage, and generating much fear. So before our journey together I want to say a few words about this side of our experience.

One of the objects in an apparently disparate collection brought to the *Road Show* was a small statue. The child's great-grandfather had travelled the world helping to build railways. This figurine came from Egypt and was several thousand years old. It was a "Shamti" – a servant buried with a dead person to help him on his journey through the nether world. Unbeknown to the boy until this moment, the object held memories of death, of sadness, of the fear of the unknown. Similarly, for us, once we allow our memories to be examined, experiences and recollections which have not troubled us in the slightest, can suddenly spring into ferocious life; thoughts we did not know are there, can spring out and frighten us, like a jack-in-the-box.

Perhaps the first thing to say is that the Shamti, small and common as in one sense it was, proved to be of considerable value. The same is true of our "dark" memories – they can be of great value and we should not avoid the whole journey "lest we discover something we cannot handle". Handling it will be helpful and health creating – and those memories which we have dismissed to a far country, may well be ones we need to reclaim. But how?

Of course, it depends exactly what they are, but essentially they are likely to focus on two kinds of realities. The first group consists of things we have done deliberately or inadvertently, directly or indirectly, which have caused harm to others. So we may be living with the consequences of suppressed guilt, anxiety, or fear lest we be discovered; or indeed the consequences of rejection, or broken relationships which flowed from them. It is vital to remember that with God there is grace to cover all our sins – not only forgiveness to wash us clean once we have faced them, confessed them, and repented of them – but grace enough to help us take hold now of that which we could not handle then. There are many dangers in seeking to run from our failures, real or imaginary, but one of the most damaging is that this process leaves us with a personal conviction that God cannot forgive all sins (because he hasn't forgiven this). We may read the Scriptures, we may preach the Scriptures, but this type of vestigial sin does a deep kind of damage to our convictions. We may not know the source of our uncertainty, we may not be at all conscious of it, but it will be doing its destructive work. It will leave us with a sense that ultimately we are not acceptable to God, that there is some kind of unspoken limit to his love for us. This will be operative even against our better judgement, but somehow, to others more perhaps than to us, the hint of darkness, the shadow across the glory of God, will be felt. But God's grace is sufficient – he can help us look again at our unspeakable mistake and gently bring it to the light of his perfect forgiveness. The light which flows from the cross is an active light that can penetrate the fibres of our memories, and erase the most ingrained and stubborn stains.

It may be helpful to share any such experience with a close and sensitive Christian friend. It may be right to meet with a minister or Christian counsellor but always remember:

> *If we say that we have no sin, we deceive ourselves, and there is no truth in us. But if we confess our sins to God, he will keep his promise and do what is right: he will forgive us our sins and purify us from all our wrongdoing. If we say that we have not sinned, we make God out to be a liar, and his word is not in us.*

1 John 1.8–10

Remember, too, that although such memories may be buried and carry the flavour of death – they are of considerable value when handled properly.

The second main category of problem memories is memories of harmful things done to us. Such experiences breed all kinds of off-spring: hatred, self-rejection, suspicion, and fear are but a few.

Here is a meditation from another source which captures the sense of fear and the kinds of difficulties that it may lead us towards.

> *Parking lot*
> * car in sight*
> *Woman carrying shopping, makes her way past*
> *two men*
> * waiting in parked car – watching*
> *Feels menacing – feels alone*
> * Try not to panic.*

> *Men, out of car – still watching*
> * Fumble for her key – hand on shoulder*
> * Men are here*

> *Horrid leering face – promise of pain – fear*
> * God, where are you? You should be here*
> * You said you would – always.*

> *Sudden start, thank God – only a dream.*
> *But God where were you? What does this mean?*
> *Lying back on the pillow, I see:*
>   *A man*
> *In a garden – waiting*
>   *Appointed time – coming soon*
> *Snaking its way up the hill an eerily lit procession.*
>   *They're coming – it's time.*
>
>   *Try not to panic*
>   *Heart-beat – quicker*
> *Suffocating fear, surrounding, blanket-like*
>   *Can't breathe.*
> *A traitor's kiss, faces of flint*
>   *Surrounded by people – completely alone.*
>   *"My God, my God, where are you?"*
> *God, where are you in times like these?*
> *Tell me, what does this mean?*
>
> *My Son, waiting in the garden*
>   *Surrounded by fear, cut off from me*
>   *Completely alone*
> *My child, in all your life, you will never be*
>   *this alone.*
> *My Son has seen to it – I will always*
>   *be here for you.*[2]

Our major difficulty, as Christians, is the sense that God wasn't there when we needed him. Often that is the way it really seems. Often we don't perceive that is the major difficulty – it may be the pain we live with, the insecurities which trap us in every relationship, the self-depreciation we hurl at ourselves every day and so on, but what a difference it would make to know God was really with us and did something about it. Here is actually one of our problems. The Christian answer is that God has done something decisively about "it" for us. The poem seems to draw in the healing power of Christ. So does the by now famous "Footprints".

So, the implication is, no matter what you felt, no matter how things seemed, you were not alone, you were not unprotected – someone bore the pain and experienced your trauma with you. What we really want, however, is that they would have borne it for us, instead of us, perhaps better still have destroyed those who threatened us and did so much damage. The cry of the tortured human heart is "Why, if you loved me and you were there as you say, why didn't you stop it?" Here is our problem; we can't change God for a god. He is the God of powerlessness, of crucifixion. He is the Father who for ever stands in the doorway longing and looking for his son to return. He is not the Father who fetches him back in an armoured personnel carrier. So, for healing to happen we need the kind of connection made in the poem. That is where I am vulnerable and helpless too – for I do not control the ministry of the Holy Spirit. Yet I want to affirm the truth of all that "The Dream" and "Footprints" poems stand for.

CHRISTMAS LIGHTS

So let me begin with a painful memory of mine from unexpected places! I have already hinted that at the time I'm writing Christmas has been happening. Christmas lights are all around – in our home, on the Christmas tree, on the television, on the Christmas cards about us. They also greet us every time we venture forth – strung from trees in gardens, framing doorways, enticing shoppers in the town centre, gleaming around pubs and restaurants. They are a sign of cheerfulness, of welcome, of music in colour and I can enjoy it all I hope. But for me, they will always carry an undercurrent of pain and sadness – for they take me back over twenty years.

It was going to be a good time. My wife and I were going to her parents for a pre-Christmas visit. My Ph.D. thesis was almost ready, we were settling well into our first church, where I was the new pastor. There was only a couple of months to wait for the birth of our first baby – a baby which we felt was especially a gift from God. We had been married four-and-a-half years. For four years my wife had worked in order to enable me to continue my advanced theological studies. Sometimes it had been hard for her but she had stuck at it, and now at the earliest possible convenient moment God had blessed us with this child she carried.

Then she began to feel pains. At least she had the comfort of her mother with all her experience to surround her. The doctor was summoned, a Christian from our old church. The ambulance was called. I followed in our car somewhat anxious, but mainly excited. After all the baby was seven-and-a-half months – that was nothing extraordinary for those days. We would have our baby for Christmas!

For a whole day I sat in a lonely hospital waiting room. The messages I received from the medical staff were very infrequent and very general, but they were not reassuring. After endless hours of separation from the woman I loved with all my heart, the woman who carried our hopes and the blessing of God, we were together again, bewildered by an incalculable sorrow, united by the anguish and pain of all she had been through. There was no baby – only a misshapen being too ill to survive in our world – there was no new life only death, there was no joy only confusion and the fear of what so much pain would do to us, and also, to all who loved us: how would we cope?

The baby was anacephalic and had hydrocephalis – words of enlightenment to the medical staff, but not to us. The baby was a boy.

After a time of consolation with each other, a time when I could catch up a little on the pain, the powerlessness, the indignity, and the lonely anguish of my wife, I set out to journey home alone. It was dark; dark inside and dark outside. Then into my darkness came an awareness of coloured lights – lights which shouted like a string of jesters, "It's Christmas". Into my mind, complete with choir and orchestra, sang the words "Unto us a boy is born". From a dark recess, so deep down I did not know it could exist within me, came a shout of defiance, intertwined with complete bewilderment. "Yes, and your son, when he was born, was all right."

Then, I suppose it was almost simultaneously but I have no way of knowing, for it came from eternity, there was a reply, firm but wrapped in the gentleness of love, "Yes, and I had to watch him die, in helpless agony".

In that moment, I understood, although not yet with my mind, that my anguish as a young father – now not to be, a husband whose love could not reach the desperation of his wife, a child returning to carry sad tidings to waiting parents-in-law, and who knows how many others, in that moment, I knew my anguish was an experience God shared with me.

So Christmas lights, a modern superficial symbol, our way of trying to be neighbourly, or to join in the celebrations, to bring cheer into the darkness of mid-winter, or even to lure us into a shopping centre, take me straight back as though time has never existed, into that moment at once so awful and so awesome. I suppose Christmas lights must carry other memories too for me, but I cannot find them.

Please don't think that moment was some kind of fairy scattering star-dust and healing the wounds painlessly. There was then, and sometimes still is, a dark stony road that had to be walked. Sorrow, anger, loneliness, conflict, confusion, momentary loss of faith, pretence, and so much more indeed on a road whose horrors and pitfalls can never be measured but only walked, a step at a time. Yet, for me, that road was always a journey with God and not against him because of that experience of transaction triggered by the first sight of Christmas lights.

I know how fortunate I am. The horror I experienced was, in some contexts, almost nothing. It was not cruelty, vindictiveness, abuse, deliberately and maliciously inflicted by someone who was supposed to love and protect me. It was not an "accident" caused by someone else's thoughtless indulgence, which left my life shattered, paralysed, twisted. Nor was I left twisted by it, for God's healing Spirit can cope whatever our pain may be. If I did not know this, I would hardly dare to write this book. It is into his hands that I commit your spirit.

AN IRON

Now for a different kind of backwards look. I wonder if you know the old song: "Running away with the smoothing iron she stole my heart away."

Ironing – some people love it. Honestly they do. They find it relaxing, rewarding, restoring. The quiet rhythm gives them a pulse, a pause for reflection from the rush and clamour of clanging spoons and electrical equipment, or peace and quiet to listen to music without feeling guilty. The pile of half-folded, crumpled clothes transformed into crisp, presentable shirts, blouses, trousers, and shirts, gives them a rich sense of achievement. Into the ironing goes love and skill, a sense of joy that they can give so much to the family whose daily presence they value.

Ironing – some people hate it. A never-ending thankless chore. Clothes seem no better when ironed than before. Creases and crinkle are pressed permanently in, instead of smoothed out. Ironing is not the end of a process, the making of all things new, but rather the start of a round of chores – for soon these same clothes will be on the conveyor belt again.

For all of us, those who use it and those who don't, the iron is a familiar object in every household. It is something we see, something we use, but also something we feel. As we hold it, it becomes an extension of our personality. But what memories does it stir?

Does it stir memories of a wedding present list perhaps? It was the gift that Aunty Mary and Uncle John ticked – but was it exactly the one you wanted – even if it was the one you ordered, was it quite what you thought it would be? Did it fill you with joy or fear as you unpacked it from its box and thought of all the years of ironing ahead of you? How did your husband react when you asked him to fix the plug – or did you do it yourself? Or, as the husband, had you already agreed to the ironing too!

Inevitably comparisons with your father and his father come to mind – inevitably comparisons with your mother and his mother pushed and pulled at your emotions.

Perhaps it holds other memories. For irons don't always do what we want, as I found out to my cost. I remember a certain prized garment of my daughter's – it didn't really need ironing – it was supposed to have a crinkled look – but to finish off the job, as the iron cooled down, I thought I would just smooth it down a little. At the first touch of the iron a hole appeared as if by magic! How foolish I was not to stick to the instructions. How would I tell my daughter, how could I compensate? How would I face my wife? Childhood inadequacies mingled with the crowd of competing emotions.

There are other childhood memories – memories of a mother ironing. When washing days were cold and wet, and the ironing board of wood, towered above my head. Then it was a small, stainless steel iron. No steam hissed from the heart. Memories, some of ease and satisfaction, some of weariness and pressure.

But I can remember other irons – dark black and small and heavy. Irons which had to be heated by the coal fire in my grandmother's house. Irons seen again in an industrial museum, turning my childhood into "history" for my child!

An iron is a cold/hot object, clinical in its lines, functional in its designs, transformed by technology in my lifetime. Yet it holds the key to many rich human memories. It is the symbol of patient loving care, of clothes worn proudly because so well pressed. Like so much of our modern world it is a piece of utilitarian technology – but capable of conveying deep and rich messages of love and tenderness.

For me it is itself a symbol of the world and God. We can either view an iron as an object, a number in an Argos catalogue, impersonal replicated a million times – or a vehicle of personal style and meaning. Elizabeth Browning captured a similar dichotomy.

> *Earth's crammed with heaven*
> *And every common bush afire with God;*
> *But only he who sees, takes off his shoes,*
> *the rest sit round it and pluck Blackberries,*
> *and daub their natural faces unaware.* [3]

Both views have their validity. But please forgive me, Lord, for the days when I am so busy an iron is only an object to be tidied out of the way and not a ticket to a world far richer in its magic than EuroDisney. Forgive me for days (for some sadly a whole lifetime) when the world is only such an object too and I miss the hands that hold the world.

> *How clearly the sky reveals God's glory!*
> *How plainly it shows what he has done!*
> *Each day announces it to the following day;*
> *each night repeats it to the next.*
> *No speech or words are used, no sound is heard;*
> *yet their message goes out to all the world*
> *and is heard to the ends of the earth.*

> Psalm 19.1–4

Before we leave our iron let me emphasize again your journey probably will be, indeed, probably should be, quite different. Your memory might be one of special privilege and pleasure – a special time when your mother gave herself to you, and with unusual (for her) patience and gentleness taught you how to iron; a time when she was encouraging and not critical; a moment in your development when you felt she was affirming you and your growth towards personhood. For another, the memories might take you to a special childhood birthday when you were given a toy iron and ironing board; maybe it was that your friend received such a present and you were seethingly jealous. For another it might be your hatred, for ironing was a punishment or it felt like an unfair chore forced on to a young teenager by hard-pressed parents or parent. For another the iron might scream of pain and fear, for their experience of irons is dominated by an accident when they were burnt by one. The point is not that our experiences must be of any one kind, but that in taking the journey backwards a multiplicity of memories will surface. Good or bad, bright or shadowy, welcomed or feared, each memory is actually part of us, it has helped to make us the person we have become and by offering such memories to God, we can become people who are being re-made after his likeness. With each memory invite him to step into it and show you where he was, and what now he wishes to do for you with that memory.

If this process seems difficult to you then perhaps some of the following suggestions may help.

Why not try writing down your experience? This has several advantages. We revisit our memories more slowly, see things in more detail, give ourselves time to feel them more vividly, and sometimes see what we normally avoid: it is often this which is the key to appreciating more fully or resolving the pain of our remembering and so discovering God's presence there.

Perhaps it will help to ask a question or two of our memories. Again it is probably a good thing to put one question at a time to our recall of past experience and having that question written in front of us may be helpful to start with.

- "Do the feelings evoked by looking back teach me something about God or myself?"

- "Are there some rich recollections that prompt me to give thanks to God? If so take time to do so.

- "Is there something in that remembered experience which clashes with the way God is supposed to be?" If so, that clash needs to be faced – it is actually a closed door keeping God out.

- "If Jesus had been visibly with you at the time, what would you have liked to say to him?" Say it now, whether it is an expression of anger, appreciation, or love. Say it, whether it is a question to be shared, a challenge you need to make, or a half-formed expression of confusion. In daring to share our questions we invite God into our past, which is, of course, part of our present.

But, please, try not to become too busy asking questions all the time. This can itself become a technique on which we depend, or even a defence mechanism to keep God away. At least, on some occasions, ask God to be with you as you recall your experiences and simply walk down memory lane with him.

A VASE

Every home has some "artistic" objects and they too are part of our modern world. For our third trip down memory lane I have chosen one of those. It is a vase standing 10 inches tall (I know I could say 25 centimetres, but that is not how it was perceived when it came into our family.) It stands on a window sill in our home, and I wish I could draw it or describe it, but I cannot do either with any kind of adequacy. All I can say is that it has a basically rectangular cross section with curved corners. The background is beige and on it are somewhat stylized leaves and flowers, in mauve and purple. It is actually a very pleasant and attractive vase – although rereading my inadequate description I know it doesn't sound it. It was my mother's vase – we have it because my mother died fourteen years ago – suddenly while we were living away – 160 miles away. But of course we didn't have it straight away – not until my father died a couple of years later. So, in some ways the memories this vase evokes is a journey of sadness, but it brings me delight to know my wife is fond of the vase too. I suppose, in a strange and largely irrational way, her willing acceptance of the vase is an affirmation of her acceptance of my parents – although all of that is somewhat difficult to unravel. Perhaps it is that she, in God's grace, among many other roles, fills the gap, or at least the edges of the gap, which the death of parents leaves.

But the attractiveness of the vase, its gentle warmth and vibrancy, is not the main reason I value it, nor indeed are the memories of my parents – rich as they are. No, the memories associated with this vase rush almost undeflected to the time of its arrival in our family. That vase is surrounded by a rich, warm, sunshine glow of friendship, love, human and divine. It was given as a gift by "the folk" (they were always "the folk") who worshipped God in a tiny methodist chapel in Leicestershire, which was my spiritual nursery. Those first nine years were basically secure, and certainly through the windows of worshipful and caring lives I absorbed a sense of God's reality, to hold me when other pressures were dragging me out into a dark and unknown sea. That was why my parents treasured that vase – it was full of something more wonderful than flowers, no matter how vivid their colour, no matter how rich their scent – it was full of well-known voices, the welcoming call of names, the whispered deeds of kindness. It was enriched, I think, by a sense that those days were days of a simpler, kinder, sweeter life, that, for my parents and probably for all, had gone for ever. Such a vase is totally irreplaceable. It is treasured beyond the power of words.

Even as I write, with a heart bursting with thankfulness for such a pure goodness a fear leaps out. How will I cope the day that vase falls to the ground and smashes? Will I turn in anger on the one whose carelessness has destroyed such beauty – knowing full well that "the one" could easily be me? Will I, by my reaction, smash the spell of love and friendship it contains, just as certainly as the dreaded thud of the pottery on the floor will smash the vase? Perhaps, but I think not – for deep within me is the knowledge that the physical object is indeed only the facade for the true riches.

Yet we who have this spiritual treasure are like common clay pots, in order to show that the supreme power belongs to God, not to us. ... For this reason we never become discouraged. Even though our physical being is gradually decaying, yet our spiritual being is renewed day after day. ... For we know that when this tent we live in – our body here on earth – is torn down, God will have a house in heaven for us to live in, a home he himself has made, which will last for ever. ... While we live in this earthly tent, we groan with a feeling of oppression; it is not that we want to get rid of our earthly body, but that we want to have the heavenly one put on over us, so that what is mortal will be transformed by life. God is the one who has prepared us for this change, and he gave us his Spirit as the guarantee of all that he has in store for us.

2 Corinthians 4.7, 16; 5.1, 4–5

Somehow such truth is captured for me in that vase. It speaks of a time in life that had to die, of parents who had to die, but only so that the one who gave life to all can give to each a richer, fully freer way of being.

Suggested Activities

1. Are there objects or situations which set off painful memories for you? Can you use them as a means of sharing your pain? If you are using this book in a group context why not suggest that each member brings an object and uses it to talk about their painful memories?

2. Equally, why not do the same for something which brings joy and brightness?

3. OK, so how do you respond to:

   (a) the iron and ironing;

   (b) or the spade and gardening;

   (c) or the chamois leather and the windows, or car etc.?

4. If you are using this book with others, share together the different kinds of question that help you listen for God and what he has to say, through your memories.

5. For those in a hurry – make a list of objects you will explore for their memory value. Carry the list with you and then, when you are kept waiting – use the list and enjoy the time, instead of enduring the frustration.

Notes

1   Quotation from *Readers' Digest*, April 1986, p. 81. For some people, and some memories, the feel is very different. Remembering hurts, crushes and paralyses. We shall take note of this, in a while.

2   Sue Bell, "The Dream" in Michele Guiness (ed.) *Tapestry of Voices* (SPCK, London, 1993), pp. 48–9.

3   Elizabeth Barrett Browning, "Aurora Leigh", Book vii.

10 LOOKING OUTWARDS

In Chapter 9, we found that certain things can help us explore our inner space. Rather like Alice in Wonderland, once we have squeezed ourselves through we find ourselves falling into another, larger world, governed by a different set of rules, not ruled by the slavery' of scientific rationalism; but there is a different yet equally enriching journey we can take using familiar objects as a key for explanation. Again we need to squeeze ourselves through an opening which at first seems constricting, but in fact leads us on into the entire world. The difference is this. We do not allow an object to trigger things in us – to open us up to ourselves, rather it is the origins of the object which prompt our journey.

The Bible itself takes quite an interest in where things have come from. This is true for Abraham, the father of the Jewish race, who leaves the city of Ur in Babylon; it is true of the stones and the cedar wood for Solomon's temple (1 Kings 6.7; 7.9–10; 1 Kings 5.8–10). More significantly the biblical drama is set within the context of the nations (e.g. Genesis 10) and the arena of redemption is the whole world (Matthew 16.18–20; Acts 1.8; 2.5–12). It is highly appropriate, then, that we should develop a sense of openness to the whole world and expect God to speak to us through this. How can we do this through the bric-à-brac around us each day? Here are some suggestions.

Most of us, once we are showered, dressed, and more or less in our right minds, face something similar each day – the cereal packet! Few things are more familiar, or more mundane, but they contain within themselves a fascinating world. Let's settle on one that has been around longer than most – the cornflake packet. Essentially it consists of three parts – the cardboard box, the white polythene bag, and the contents. It's nothing much to get worked up about. We could journey down memory lane – do you remember the waxed paper before polythene was invented, the ways people used that in the aftermath of the Second World War when things were in short supply etc.? But that is not our chosen path today.

We could, I suppose, explore the world of technology and manufacture – for each part of the cornflake packet. I am sure there are some who would find that a fascinating journey – and nothing is out of bounds – yet that is not the way we are exploring together at this point. Rather I simply want us to journey to the source of origin of the raw materials. The cardboard comes from pulp and the pulp comes from soft wood forests. We can take our journey to Canada or Norway to visit hectares of spruce trees growing on endless hillsides, giving bright lustre to the vision of tourists who drive by, shade to the animals who, flying or walking, use these trees for their habitat. So, we can thank God for those who, for commercial reasons no doubt, work in cold and heat to plant, protect, thin out, spray for disease and insects, wait patiently, and eventually harvest the green giants which end up as the packing in "my" cornflake box. Without hope and stability few companies, let alone people, plant forests, even for pulp. Yet if people did not plant for the future we know we would soon run out of cornflake packets! Interwoven with the mountainous beauty of a forest and the commercial organization which requires it, is an unquantifiable but essential ingredient for the cycle of paper manufacture – hope – a future look. How is it that such immaterial "realities" are necessary to sustain our secular materialism? Cornflake packets reveal the interwovenness of the material and the spiritual.

The polythene bag is less obvious than the eye-catching packet, but so necessary if the cornflakes are to land in my dish not only clean but crunchy crisp. Where does that come from? Polythene certainly doesn't grow on trees! Although in a rather remote sense I suppose it does. Polythene is one of the multitudinous commodities for which we need oil, and oil comes from subterranean sources, the result of millions of years of forestation, compressed and caught by the movements of the earth's crust. Such quiet, unassuming, flexible material is not possible without the investment of millennia and the violence of geological upheavals. But that is not the only violence which springs into my mind at the thought of oil. Before my eyes are the vivid pictures of deserts with oil wells bursting raw red flames, disgorging dark, toxic fumes – the final scenes from a real-life film of war and calculated destruction that we know simply as the Gulf War. Overlaying the flames are glimpses of haunted, hopeless Iraqi troops surrendering with a pitiful relief, to Americans, and washing round the footage of convoys of human defeatedness are thick, oily waves slurping on a dark beach, conveying the reluctant carnage of dead seabirds. Who knows how much oil had to do with Iraq's invasion of Kuwait and the rapid response of the West? Certainly without oil in many forms such a war could not have been fought. And without oil, the clinical white polythene which keeps my cornflakes in ever pristine condition could not have been manufactured. So, I weep, quietly, inwardly, for the complexity of a world I cannot unravel and dare not live without. Somewhere within me there is a desperate cry for help and, although exegetically no doubt it is inappropriate, the caverns of my mind echo with the desolation. "Wretched man that I am, who can deliver me from the body of death?"

But in the bowl, still glinting with the sunshine it seems, a different journey beckons me. For the cornflakes, to the British an unfortunate misnomer, come from those yellow pea-like grains of maize. They tell of months of rapid growth, of greenery in fertile alluvial plains, well watered by life-giving rains or carefully monitored irrigation systems. Tall, green, giant shoots, filling out daily with sheaths of seed, seed that, absorbing the bronze, relentless sun, itself becomes sunlike in colour. An energy transfer of incredible complexity turns the immaterial rays of the sun into solid pellets. Cornflakes speak of fields of thriving, growing maize, daily moving towards harvest time, bathed in glorious sunshine, moving in a slow waltz to the prompting of the wind. It speaks to a body and a soul about to dash, rush, push, and strive, about waiting, maturing, becoming what we are receiving. Cornflakes invite us to gaze into deep pools of gold and to learn to see our reflection, and be still and safe.

I waited patiently for the Lord's help;
then he listened to me and heard my cry.
He pulled me out of a dangerous pit,
out of the deadly quicksand.
He set me safely on a rock and made me secure.
He taught me to sing a new song, a song of praise to our God.
Many who see this will take warning and will put their trust
in the Lord.

Happy are those who trust the Lord,
who do not turn to idols
or join those who worship false gods.
You have done many things for us, O Lord our God;
there is no one like you!

You have made many wonderful plans for us.
I could never speak of them all –
their number is so great!
...

Lord, I know you will never stop being merciful to me.
Your love and loyalty will always keep me safe.

Psalm 40.1–5, 11

You, Lord, are all I have,
and you give me all I need;
my future is in your hands.
How wonderful are your gifts to me;
how good they are!

I praise the Lord, because he guides me,
and in the night my conscience warns me.
I am always aware of the Lord's presence;
he is near, and nothing can shake me.

And so I am thankful and glad,
and I feel completely secure,
because you protect me from the power of death,
I have served you faithfully,
and you will not abandon me to the world of the dead.

You will show me the path that leads to life;
your presence fills me with joy
and brings me pleasure for ever.

Psalm 16.5–11

So, the simple cornflake packet unfolds several mysteries as fascinating and complex as the unfurling of a rose. Put all three together and the story becomes yet more complex. Add to them the design, manufacture, transportation, and sales procedure that enable them to be on my breakfast bar – add to these the stories of international trade, of finance and currency markets, of human management skills and ultimately human trust, without which everything else breaks down. Then I begin to marvel at the wonderful gift I so easily take for granted. They provide me with unlimited opportunity for travel, for commercial exploration, for scientific discovery. Sometimes these reflective journeys will make me glad, sometimes bring sorrow and repentance for the evil people have done to each other. Sometimes I will catch the fragrance of the divine image in which we are made as I see the invisible realities of hope, trust, courage, kindness. On other occasions I will end up face to face with human cruelty and even of satanic oppression as I glimpse again the viciousness which also exists. Each moment of discovery through the familiar objects around me is an opportunity to meet with God at the intersection of his world.

In some ways most of what I am discovering and seeking to share in this chapter was summed up by a seventeenth-century poet George Herbert. He wrote some very complex and profound poetry, with very involved metaphors and rhyme schemes, obscure allusions, and somewhat fanciful patterns with the length of his lines. Here for instance is a stanza from his poem "Easter Wings":

> *Lord who createst man in wealth and store*
> *Though foolishly he lost the same,*
> *Decaying more and more*
> *Till he became*
> *Most poore:*
> *with Thee*
> *O let me rise,*
> *As larks, harmoniously,*
> *And sing this day Thy victories:*
> *Then shall the fall further the flight in me.*

The second half of this complex poem summarizes what we are seeking to do in meditation. However George Herbert also wrote often with a deceptive simplicity and some of his poems have become familiar to us as hymns. Again this helps us both to explore another familiar object – glass, but also, as we do first, to understand something more about Christian Meditation.

> *A man that looks on glass*
> *on it may stay his eye*
> *Or, if he pleases, through it pass*
> *And then the heavens espy.*

Sometimes, as we look out towards the garden on a sunny day, especially one at the end of a long winter, we are very conscious of all the rain smudges left by the lashing water which has deposited minute particles of dust that may have travelled all the way from the Sahara, or only from the incinerator half-a-mile away. We can see the fingerprints of mischievous children, whose sticky hands deposited a trace of sweetness on the glass. Even the slight imperfections left in the glass when it was manufactured, or through wear and tear, are noticeable in the glinting sun. So we can decide it is time to get the chamois leather out. Or, we can see beyond to the daffodils glinting gold in the borders and the verdant tulip leaves promising their rainbow of colours soon to appear. Then we decide it is time to get the hoe out and to start enhancing the borders. George Herbert might also have had another kind of glass in mind – the mirror. For George Herbert was very conscious that humankind is made in God's image. So, he may have been suggesting that as we look at ourselves we may either stay with our own reflection, with all its familiarity and imperfections, or we may see beyond to the heavenly dimension of life which we represent.

Whichever interpretation of George Herbert's imagery is correct, the poem now directs us to the fascinating qualities of glass. Even today it is a frequent presence in our lives. Glass is used for containers for jam and milk, for wine and pickles (and this in spite of the plastic revolution). It is a cheap and common material, yet one that can be used to create tremendous beauty. On our silver wedding anniversary we visited the Caithness factory in Oban, Scotland. There, from very ordinary materials of mainly sand, with a few metallic oxides to add glowing colours, mixed with the enormous heat of the glass furnaces and the skills of the craftworkers, solid paperweights with intriguing, gossamer-like wisps of sculptured elegance captured inside, are created. Whether it is plate glass for domestic windows, crystal glass for elegant wine glasses, or the heavy stuff of paperweights, it is essentially the same. Who would have imagined that the dull, dry desert sand could be so useful, so creative, so beautiful? But not without using vast amounts of energy to change its chemical structures. As I think of glass, I think of human beings.

> *"What is man?" questions the psalmist.*
> *"You were made from soil" God proclaims.*

That is about it – less than £1 worth of basic common elements, mainly carbon and water, with a few additional trace elements. But with divine fusion what an incredible variety of forms and shapes have been produced. What variety of purpose and gifts, and who knows the limits that are set for us? But in the process of our making both skill and warmth have been infused.

> *A man that looks on glass*
> *on it may stay his eye…*

So, as I see all kinds of glass around me, mostly very ordinary, some decorative, but mainly functional, I give thanks to God for the creative potential of ordinary materials and I ask that he will help me always to look beyond the common place or even "special" people, both to the materials from which we are made and the creative genius of the one who made us.

God also speaks to me through another quality which glass possesses. It is brittle and therefore breakable. Plate glass needs to be protected by a frame which prevents it from being bent. Tumblers need to be packed in cartons to preserve them in transit, the candle holder needs to be steady on the wooden shelf, away from the risk of being easily dislodged. The very qualities which make glass such a serviceable material are the ones which make it vulnerable to destruction. I ask God to remind me of this in all my dealings with people. They may appear strong and resistant, and in many ways they are; but all of us have our vulnerability, it is partly the materials from which we are made and partly a necessary entailment of being what we are.

Of course, we can follow the materials from which the glass is made back to their places of origin too, as we did for the cornflakes and their package, but I will leave you to make that journey outwards for yourself, if you so wish.

But now let me take you on another journey. My wife likes arranging flowers. Often for a present, to express appreciation or to share in someone's special celebration, she will create a beautiful synthesis of colour, shape, and texture which will bring much delight and satisfaction. The flowers are normally placed in "oasis", fascinating material I am sure, and the oasis in a basket. It is those baskets which provide the focus for our next mental travel. Baskets, of all shapes and sizes and made from a considerable variety of materials, but mainly from grasses and cane, have made a real comeback in recent years. But where do these baskets come from?

They come partly from the concern of organizations like Oxfam, Christian Aid, and Traidcraft, to provide families in the developing world with the opportunity to start providing for their needs and so to create for them a greater sense of dignity and worth. But where are these grasses and canes grown? A couple of verses from the Bible give us a clue:

*When she saw what a fine baby he was, she hid him for
three months. But when she could not hide him any longer,
she took a basket made of reeds and covered it with tar to
make it watertight.*

Exodus 2.2–3

The natural place for such material is in the wet and warm places
of the world like the Nile Delta. Today many of them come from
appropriate parts of Africa, China, and Bangladesh.

Baskets make such a refreshing change from boxes and
polythene bags, and all the other vehicles we use to package and
carry things in. "Why is that?" I ask myself. I suspect it is
something to do with the richer variety of shapes that can be
created. Probably it is also to do with the more human sense they
carry because of the skill and energy invested in them. But it is also
the materials from which they are made. They have spent their
growing time wafting in the cool breezes of the evening. They have
responded vigorously to the power of the burning sun as they have
spurted in growth. They have been harvested and cleaned. But they
must be woven while they are wet. Sometimes the materials will
have been soaked to make them supple again, sometimes before
they have dried out fully they will have been woven skilfully into
patterns that weave in the past creativity of the generations.

Each of those countries warrants our prayers. Perhaps for a
country like China whose structures have been fixed by the dogmas
of Marxism and the control of the political machine, we can pray
that God's spirit will continue to soften the organizational
structures again. We glimpse this happening through a partial
openness to Western (or Eastern) capital investment and the trials
of the free market economy in some parts. We may rejoice in
the rapid growth of the Christian community. Such glimpses
encourage us to soak this vast country in prayer that all its people
become pliable and open to the love of God in Christ Jesus. We
may recognize that if this happens then the patterns of church life
and the understanding of the Gospel there will be different from
those in the West.

The basket shapes will involve not only pliable materials, but
will also integrate local and oriental sensitivities. Then our lives
will be enriched by the flow of understanding and commitment, as
indeed is already happening. The outward journey through the
basket may prompt us to pray thankfully for people like
Hudson Taylor who founded the China Inland Mission, or may

remind us to pray for organizations like Open Doors which seek to make the Scriptures available in countries like this today. Perhaps too, as we catch our clothes on the roughness of the basketry, or even stab a finger with a broken stem, we will be called to pray for the suffering of the Church in China.

Again, there are many ways in which the journey outwards, that is of discovering something of the materials from which things are made, can prove a stimulus to prayer and may be a channel for God to speak in a more personal way. Baskets, such as the ones I have in mind, are cheap and disposable, even though their manufacture may well have involved many hours of cheap labour. I need to check that I do not allow my attitude to the baskets to become the model of my attitude to the Chinese! I need to remember, God says, that each one of the vast millions is made to be his child; each one is a distinct person, created by God and loved by God; made for a deeply intimate relationship with him, made too for friendship in Christ with me.

All around us, then, are objects we often take for granted, whose materials can lead us to all parts of the world and, as we do so, can become prompts for living conversation with God. For some of these objects we may need to investigate the origins of their materials. God may speak to us through the objects we investigate, through the issues and needs he highlights, as we discover more about their make-up and the countries from which they come. But, of course, he may speak in a clearly personal and distinctive way as he creates his special synthesis between ordinary materials and ourselves.

Suggested Activities

1. Ask God what everyday items he would like you to explore in the ways suggested by this chapter. Perhaps you will need to do some research – visit the library and find out about the materials and the countries from which they come – then contact missionary societies which operate in those countries to find out about the Christian Church there. The Evangelical Missionary Alliance (at Whitefield House, 186 Kennington Park Road, London SE11 4BT) may be able to help. Or you can use Patrick Johnstone's *Operation World, Operation Mobilisation*, 1993.

2. How does this kind of exploration make you feel? How does it prompt you to pray? Can you sense how God feels towards people in those countries, working in those conditions, using their resources?

3. To what extent do human responses like fear, bitterness, envy, trust, co-operation, and hope contribute to the economies and technology of our world? You may find the pictorial representation of the cost of sin to the world helps you to handle the negative side of this equation.

In God's world...

- Just over 30% of the gross world product is related to the "structures of sin".

- The total cost of the "structures of sin" every year is $5.2 trillion.

- The great majority of the activities which constitute the "structures of sin" are done by the affluent and the well-off.

- It is estimated that $520 billion per year would be sufficient to provide the world's poor with adequate food, water, education and shelter.

Taken originally from B. L. Myers, *The Changing Shape of World Mission* (California, 1993), p. 34. Redrawn by Mike Dilly, Bible Society.

11 LOOKING AWAY

THE DENTIST

Chapter 10 was an opportunity for armchair travel. It helped us to recognize the wonder and to investigate the personal, spiritual significance of the contents of objects and familiar "bits and bobs" in our lives. For me, at any rate, the discovery of this particular dimension to my life adds a great deal of awareness, and enriches my sense of privilege, appreciation, and responsibility before God. I realize with a new keenness that I am living within the bounty of the whole world brought to my home. But this growing sense of depth, significance, and meaning is not restricted to objects around me and the practicalities of everyday life. Nor is the awareness of God and his conversations with me limited to these aspects of life. I have discovered the same challenging communication can happen as we leave the home to make visits and share in events. To put it another way, it would be a pity, indeed an unnecessary tragedy, if we only learnt to discover God in the static objects and familiar surrounding of our home territory. He is available to us in the changing environment of our daily encounters.

Before I attempt to involve you with me in this aspect of meditation I would like to underline an obvious point. I have not discovered the sense of God in the world around me all at once. It has taken several years. One of the dangers of reading through a book like this is that so many new approaches are being suggested that we end up with "overload" and the whole process becomes counterproductive. So, if there is any part of you saying "Oh no, not another one!", please give yourself time and space to rest, so as to enjoy discovering God's conversations with you in ways that have already been helpful. Unless you lose it, this book will still be available to help you when you are ready for more! It does take time to appropriate the insights contained in each chapter. We need not only to understand what is being said, but discover how it works for us; each of us is different. Then we have to start coming to terms with all that God is saying to us. So do stop and pause for weeks, if necessary, with any "style" that suits you before leaping into the next section. Equally, do feel free to leave any chapter or part of a chapter, if it comes across as hard or difficult. Forget it for now, don't feel guilty or that in some way "I've failed". It is much better to move on swiftly until you sense, "Here at last is something for me".

However, if you are comfortable, then it is time to journey on together.

In many ways the Scriptures describe a people on the move. This is true in a spiritual sense, but also at a literal level. The concept of the pilgrim people is a very pervasive and powerful one, thoroughly applicable to both Israel and the new people of God. From many angles the mobile ark can be considered a more appropriate symbol for God's presence than the static temple. When God became resident on earth, it was in a human being who is recorded as continuously on the move (e.g. Mark 1.38) and the disciples found they encountered God powerfully when they moved on (e.g. Luke 10.1, 17). We too can gain in our relationship with God as we move through our day.

So, let's start our looking "away from home" by making a visit to the dentist. This is one place most of us go to at least twice a year. (If we don't then maybe we should either thank God for the gift of amazingly good teeth, or leave this book and make a prompt appointment – for the good of our teeth and our spirit!) For some of us it is a solitary visit and for others a family affair. I go alone. I suppose in some way it would take the loneliness away if I went with the rest of the family but I am not sure whether I would find it tolerable, coping with their anxiety when we set off and their glee when we returned; it always seems I need more dental work than the rest. Anyway, for me it is always a solitary visit and essentially it is an occasion of vulnerability.

I wonder how it is for you? Do you recall your last visit? Was there anything special for you? Did you go in pain seeking relief, or did you go with a quiet mouth fearing that cavities would be enraged by the fiery probe of steel? Were your worst fears founded, or did you leave, telling yourself that you knew you would be all right? Perhaps we can recall our first visit as a child. Certainly the quality of service provided by the dental profession has improved enormously and I am very grateful. I realize that when I started my dental history, arrangements were infinitely better than 40 years earlier still. Maybe, inevitably, as we set out for the dentist we also recall our worst visit. I have to admit that I have not had any really horrific experiences, or even occasions that were noticeably worse than average. I have always had, as far as I can judge, good dentists. Indeed, for several years my dentist was a special friend as well as a competent practitioner. In spite of all this, my visits to the dentist are essentially experiences of vulnerability.

Dentists have done as much as they can to make my experience a positive one. There is a pleasant reception area, with a smiling receptionist. The waiting room is light and provided with comfortable chairs. The tropical fish tank is placed in the psychologically correct place where there is an opening reminding me that I am not trapped in the room but free to leave. Gentle music soothes my anxieties. Inevitably, there is a large collection of bygone magazines, to allow all patients the mutual pretence that we have no more on our minds than holidaymakers on a sun-soaked beach – but try as we will we cannot lose ourselves in short stories or magazine pictures. I appreciate all the care and attempt to pacify my raging anxiety, which I am more or less managing to keep a centimetre below the eruption level.

Yet only one thing in that room really helps. It is a beautifully framed cartoon. The picture is of a tiny, frightened man, sitting in a huge, angular dentist's chair, surrounded by a collection of metal objects which would not be out of place in the local garage! Why does this monstrously unfair depiction help? Because it captures for me my sense of utter vulnerability and suggests that maybe, just perhaps, the dentist understands the emotions of the "must be calm at all costs" man who will soon move smoothly (I hope), enter the surgery and take my place confidently in the chair.

How is it I arrive in that chair, after an eternal wait of six-and-a-half minutes, that I can suddenly (but not unexpectedly) feel denuded of all my freedom; how can I feel so threatened to be controlled by another person (kind and helpful as in fact she is); how can I feel so powerless? Why does it seem that I am at her mercy? What will she discover as she searches with mirror and probes into the recesses of my mouth? Do I hope she will find the cavity where my tongue has located a problem for the last three weeks, or do I hope, as I now think, that it was all my imagination? Do I want to be relieved of pain or do I want to avoid the indignity and pain (minimized of course by injections, a reclining chair, and good customer relations) of dental fillings?

So the state of my teeth is reported in a strange code to the waiting scribe. As far as I can glimpse from my disadvantaged position she writes down all this information with a disinterested face and a scientific hand. Then comes the verdict from the judge! The person who, for a few minutes of my life only, has, it seems, absolute authority, control, and power over my destiny as well as my dentistry.

What does it feel like to walk free at the end of the visit? Unusually for me, I hardly care what it costs. I can go, return to the normal world where I walk upright and decide when, if at all, I open my mouth, and where strangers are not allowed to come anything like as close to me as the dentist did. Yet somehow it seems odd to be let out again. I leave with a weird sense of disorientation, as though I have at that moment woken up from months of hibernation. Why is it all like this?

Who else, I wonder, in God's world feels, as I have just felt in the dentist's chair? What about the mentally ill, struggling with an incoherent world of confusion inside and out? Those who have suffered and still suffer cruelty and pitiless abuse? Prisoners whose lives are dominated by other people's power? Is it like this for people who go through the regular humiliation of visiting the Department of Social Security, never knowing what kind of reception they will receive and, even when it is considerate and non-condescending, feeling totally disadvantaged? Is it like this for those who visit the bank, needing a generous overdraft facility in order to keep that small business – the sum total of their investment, of their courage, their skill, their commitment and their integrity – alive? Is it like this for people who, drawn by friendship or some other force they do not understand, enter, not knowing why they have come, our church?

There, or elsewhere when I am with people, do I do all in my power to help them feel free and affirmed, or do I, deliberately or unwittingly, reduce people to pulp, as the dentist's waiting room affects me? If I, a reasonably well-adjusted, socially competent adult person can feel like this, what of others whose self-esteem and sense of worth has been eroded or was never there? Is this how life is, constantly, for them? Is this how life is for children, at least for many children who do not experience the protection of loving, sacrificing, trustworthy parents?

How do I make childhood for my children and for the many other children that my life touches? Can my experience of total vulnerability, unfair to the dentist as it undoubtedly is, help me to understand the responses of other people to me, when they see me as an authority figure? Can I at least "put up a picture", give them a sign which lets them know I do understand? I, like them, am only made of dust.

Is this how God felt when he entered our world as a baby? Just how did Jesus face the prospect of such vulnerability as he waited in the anteroom of heaven? Was he glad to step through the doorway of incarnation, relieved that at last the ordeal was under way and there was no turning back?

Is this how people feel about God, people who have had a "bad experience of him", or who have come to hold on to a distorted and wrong view of God?

> *My God, my God, why have you abandoned me?*
> *I have cried desperately for help,*
> *but still it does not come.*
> *During the day I call to you, my God,*
> *but you do not answer;*
> *I call at night but get no rest...*
>
> *But I am no longer a man; I am a worm,*
> *despised and scorned by everyone!*
> *All who see me jeer at me;*
> *they stick out their tongues and shake their heads...*
> *My strength is gone,*
> *gone like water spilt on the ground.*
> *All my bones are out of joint;*
> *my heart is like melted wax.*
> *My throat is as dry as dust,*
> *and my tongue sticks to the roof of my mouth.*
> *You have left me for dead in the dust.*

Psalm 22.1–4, 6–7, 14–15

My visit to the dentist – all over in half-an-hour – raises for me profound and deep issues which open me up to many new dimensions and offer me fresh experiences of God. I would prefer not to go to the dentist, but I realize that without such awareness, my sensitivities would be greatly impoverished. I need to be reminded of my vulnerability and powerlessness. The psalmist knows this well.

> *You tell us to return to what we were;*
> *you change us back to dust.*
> *A thousand years to you are like one day;*
> *they are like yesterday, already gone,*
> *like a short hour in the night.*
> *You carry us away like a flood;*
> *we last no longer than a dream.*

We are like weeds that sprout in the morning,
that grow and burst into bloom,
then dry up and die in the evening.

Psalm 90.3–6

But I also need to know and experience my security. This too the same psalmist expresses clearly.

O Lord, you have always been our home.
Before you created the hills
or brought the world into being,
you were eternally God,
and will be God for ever...

Fill us each morning with your constant love,
so that we may sing and be glad all our life.

Psalm 90.1–2, 14

If I need to know this, how much more do others also? How much do we all need to meet with Jesus, who says again, and again, "Peace be with you"? (John 20.19, 21, 26).

THE SUPERMARKET

A completely different experience is provided by a visit to the super-market. According to some pundits, Descartes' principle "I think therefore I am" has been replaced by a new maxim, "I shop therefore I am". Certainly the power to purchase has become an important factor in our society, and certainly too the supermarket is the appropriate symbol for our commercialism and consumerism. Shopping is in many ways, if not the ground of being (God), the ground of our being (self-worth) – that is the occupation which seems to focus our reality for us, in a way that little else can manage. Research suggests that shopping is now the number one leisure activity. This is in marked contrast with twenty years ago, and particularly for men this is a complete change around. Much of this is due, I think, not primarily to a growing materialism and avarice, but to the hard work, ingenuity, applied psychology, and care which have been poured relentlessly into the shopping business. Great pains have been taken to make shopping a pleasing experience. So what happens on the weekly trip to the supermarket? What on earth has this to do with a relationship with God?

When you go shopping do you make a list or do you just get on and go? On the whole we "just go" although we make a mental list as we journey. Our favourite supermarket has very recently moved sites, reducing it from pole position. The journey is now more confusing than trying to ski a downhill slalom might be when you don't understand the markers! We have to negotiate so many chicanes of traffic lights that our arrival in a parking space is in itself a miracle. No doubt it would be easier in daylight, but night time journeys are a minor nightmare. Nevertheless we arrive and the bright lights of "Vanity Fare" allure us. First, however, we must arm ourselves with the necessary weapon for defence and attack – a shopping trolley. Without a trolley there is no way to push through the sprawling jungle of other shoppers! It even makes the shopping easier! Fortunately the days seem to have gone when every trolley had square wheels that went in different directions, transferring the shakes to your arms as you struggled round the shelves with tight corners. Now all runs smoothly, including the revolving door – although there are times when I feel I am walking willingly into a Venus flytrap! But now we have negotiated the modern equivalent of the drawbridge and all we need to do is keep walking and keep shopping; our existence depends on it!

There is a wonderful array of goods – fresh vegetables ensure that detours are made – rather like the steel balls in a pin-ball game, we find ourselves gently cascaded from side to side collecting packets and pots, tins and boxes, as we continue down the shelves. This is the real life – we feel for a few moments – we'll have four of these, it's cheaper if we do. That's not on the list but it's such a good buy we can't resist. So many varieties of pasta, we could do with one of each but we'd better not. Washing powder, normal, biological, new, micro, brand names by the dozen – each analysed into its cost per 100 grammes as though that made the choice any easier – trying to select the right washing powder sends the head spinning like clothes in the automatic washer! The only way to choose is to choose the same as last week – if we can find it. So on we go, toiletries and food, fresh bread, canned, frozen – and with all the money we've gained on collective bargains, best buys and everyday savers, we can surely afford to treat ourselves to a fresh cream cake or a few other luxuries.

Of course, like everyone else, we stick to our list. Well, almost (that's the advantage of a mental list!). By the time we arrive home we will have gathered all the things we went for, apart perhaps from one or two which slipped through our grasp as we bounced across the aisles, enticed by new attractive packaging, and that other one because the layout had been changed to ensure we visit everywhere including the shelves of dog food and cat litter when we have no pets.

There are many skills the supermarket shopper needs – a good eye, strong wrists to steer the trolley through the traffic jam of other trolleys, patience, decisiveness, a tall reach, a supple back to grasp down low, a steady hand to take one jar and not send the 143 others scattering to the ground. Sometimes we need great courage to face the supermarket manageress when the treacle has landed on the floor, setting glass splinters in the viscous gold, which now looks so sickly on the pale green tiles. But in the end the customer must always be right, so all is well.

All is well because an army of silent workers dressed alike, like bees, returning to the hive laden with valuable pollen collected in distant fields, toil to disgorge their bounty on the shelves for us to collect into our steel stomachs. All is well until that trolley is reaching the over-full state, when ingenuity in building construction with incompatible shapes and sizes, becomes a quickly learnt art. All is well, until the shopping is done, we scan the 24 check-outs for the smallest queue, only to find that more than 6 items eliminates you from its services. All is well until the queue in which you choose to stand means your trolley is blocking the walkway – you dare not leave a gap lest someone sneaks into your place; you dare not stand in position lest other people's trolleys and your ankles prove to be painfully incompatible. All is well until your check-out machine runs out of paper while you stand and other queues rush down like water in the plughole. All is well until you try and repack the goods again into the trolley and they will not fit. Yes, all is well for all these goods, and the very essence of life costs nothing – or so it seems – only the mere passage of a plastic rectangle through an electronic ravine. Then we are free to go, out of Aladdin's cave into the dark night, to find the car, pack the boot, to drive home, to unpack the car, to try and find a home for all those things.

What has all this to do with me and God? Let me work backwards – like playing pass the parcel – and try to unravel some of the hidden moments in the process. Why is all this hard work now considered such a pleasurable experience?

There is, for me, a satisfaction in arriving home with supplies enough for the next few days. This is partly the satisfaction appropriate to any mission accomplished, but probably has overtones of returning from the hunt with slain beast across my shoulders. It has something to do with providing the resources for my family. We have, at least, the raw materials for survival and festivity. I think this feeling is one that links me to my heavenly Father. Once home I am no longer naïve enough to believe the fantasy that the supermarket has created, "'here' is life in all its fullness". Nevertheless, I am grateful for the privilege of being able to provide for a family I love and care for. For me, the return from the supermarket is a kind of sacrament for his care and for mine. It is only a symbol, not the reality, yet a true symbol which partakes in some of the reality too. For we need food, we need soap, and we do need tin foil, for the corporate life we share. We need so much more, certainly we do, but here is a sign of all we need – security, love, hope, relationships, togetherness, and our belonging to one another and to God. I believe God takes satisfaction in providing for his children – he has given us a good world to enjoy and as I come to terms with this primordial sense, I know I am in touch with him who made me in his image. I am truly grateful to God who made me, gave me them, and gave them me.

There is another experience which is fundamental to supermarket shopping. It is a mixture of freedom and power. (No wonder I prefer it to the dentist's chair!) As we move around the aisles I am free to pick up, to clasp, to release into my trolley anything I choose to take. The whole world is at my disposal. No one will stop me taking anything. I can fill my trolley with tins of sardines or cream cakes; with tights or tomatoes – no one would stop me, no one would question – apart, that is, from my wife who walks beside me! Not only do I have such freedom, I have the power. There is, I know, a moment of reckoning to come – when I reach the till – but even that seems more imaginary than real, especially now that even cheques have given way to plastic money. One day accounts will have to tally, but in the warm, secure world of the supermarket all seems possible and within my power. Such an experience brings me near to God but also shows me how far away from him I can so easily be. Such freedom, such power is real enough, but only within the confines of the aisles of commodities. My choice is vast, but actually restricted to the produce "they" select. I can have anything I want, as long as "they" want to sell it to me. It is easy to "sell my birthright for a pot of bean soup" (compare Genesis 25.27–34).

The supermarket experience is also a sacramental warning of the dangers of living in a consumer led world. What is my value in such a world? I am of little more value than my purchasing power. I am there to be manipulated and persuaded to part with as much of my wealth as possible. I exist to maximize the shareholders' profits, to ensure they outsell their rivals down the road. Is that what I want my life to become – something fed through the grinder of commerce? If not I need God's help to keep "my going out and coming in". It is facile to think that when I leave the supermarket I escape from the tyranny of a supermarket kind of world. Rather, I live in a nightmare world where every time I escape from one, I find myself in an even larger, still more impersonal megastore; the exit from that leads only to still larger worlds – "home worlds", "business worlds", "food worlds". Bright mega prisons – unless I can hold more firmly to the God who made me to relate to people, to have contact and encounter not only contingent relations.[1] Only God is ultimately strong enough to give me my identity, to lead me into freedom and power. What Jesus said in response to Pilate I need him to say to those who drain away my real life.

Pilate said to Jesus,

> *"You will not speak to me? Remember, I have the authority to set you free and also to have you crucified." Jesus answered, "You have authority over me only because it was given to you by God."*

John 19.10–11

My only place of true security and freedom is in him who has defeated the principalities and powers, who is himself the one who dispenses with and disposes of power and authority.

> *Lord, your constant love reaches the heavens;*
> *your faithfulness extends to the skies.*
> *Your righteousness is towering like the mountains;*
> *your justice is like the depths of the sea.*
> *People and animals are in your care.*
> *How precious, O God, is your constant love!*
> *We find protection under the shadow of your wings.*
> *We feast on the abundant food you provide;*
> *you let us drink from the river of your goodness.*
> *You are the source of all life,*
> *and because of your light we see the light.*

Psalm 36.5–9

Hear my cry, O God;
listen to my prayer!
In despair and far from home
I call to you!

Take me to a safe refuge,
for you are my protector,
my strong defence against my enemies.
...

I depend on God alone;
I put my hope in him.
He alone protects and saves me;
he is my defender,
and I shall never be defeated.
My salvation and honour depend on God;
he is my strong protector;
he is my shelter.

Trust in God at all times, my people.
Tell him all your troubles,
for he is our refuge.

Human beings are all like a puff of breath;
great and small alike are worthless.
Put them on the scales, and they weigh nothing;
they are lighter than a mere breath.
Don't put your trust in violence;
don't hope to gain anything by robbery;
even if your riches increase,
don't depend on them.

More than once I have heard God say
that power belongs to him
and that his love is constant.
You yourself, O Lord, reward
everyone according to his deeds.

Psalms 61.1–3; 62.5–12

The psalmists learnt important lessons and we need to learn them too, so that we can live in a world-turned-megabowl.

Both of these "experiences" through the supermarket visit are somewhat "heavy". Sometimes there are others of a lighter nature, which are equally valid. For instance, there is the surprise and joy of discovering, among all the gleaming stainless steel racks, stacked neatly with well-ordered merchandise, among the motorway lines of trolleys, driven by anonymous humanoids, friendly faces of neighbours or people you really like from church. There is the joy of being reminded that the impersonal world of modern merchandising is actually populated with real people who smile and sneeze, who have feelings and thoughts and histories, people who have grown up with you, and who talk with their own peculiarities of dialect and inflection which make them instantly recognizable and endear them to us. Out of all the impersonal world there springs, "jack-in-the-box" like, a sense of wonderful humanity, as both sides recognize the stranger in the crowd. There is the even more stunning moment of recognition when one of the worker bees, filling the shelves, stands upright, with face alert, and you know she too is a friend, in whose house you have chatted, and whose children come running and skipping through your mind. Such moments, if not exactly of intimacy, at least of the rediscovery of humanity, are of value in themselves, but can be a crisp, kick-like reminder of the other, hidden levels of relatedness which every human being has – even those who trundle trolleys with determined aggression and acquisitiveness towards you – for they too are made to relate to the creator God. Such moments are a call to prayer "I have not stopped giving thanks to God for you" (Ephesians 1.16) and a cause for prayer – to pray for all "these people" that they might move and be moved towards God and not away from him, that they might not become like soldiers of old, imprisoned in a suit of armour made up of baked bean cans and squash bottles!

Then there are the unexpected moments of helpfulness, such as the time when being tall I can reach the topmost packet on the top shelf and pass it to a woman desperate to reach it, defeated by her 5 feet 2 inches, or the other kind of time when the very product I need has been replaced with a cavernous vacuum, but a perceptive manageress, who was fortuitously wandering along, recognizes the look of panic on my face and says – "Wait a minute, I'll get it for you". Good as her word she returns promptly and with the right product. Overwhelming gratitude suggests that I should take a box full, but so far, perhaps disappointingly, common sense prevails and I take just one packet. These are moments of unnecessary but fulfilling generosity, moments that have recognized another's need and rushed to meet it. Pale reflections they may be, but they are glimpses nevertheless of the attitude of our Father.

Humour is not entirely absent from the supermarket either. There is, as far as I know, no official highway code for trolleys and while at times that can lead to titanic clashes of strength, steel, and will, it can also lead to dance somewhat akin to courting birds! No matter which way we weave our trolley, the oncoming one has already moved there too. It seems we shall be forever in one another's way. Yet there is no room for anger as both parties recognize the silliness. So a silent breakthrough into friendship almost occurs. Sometimes I think God plays such trolley games with us. I recall moments when my own gyrations to avoid him having failed utterly I have at last surrendered, only to sense his loving kindness.

I can in no way predict the basket full of special memories you trundle away with you from the supermarket visits, but I am sure many of them have the potential, when unwrapped, to bring God a little nearer to you, as so often they have done, for me. Not all will be like the one I have described. Certainly many do not start off this way. Often I go with a weariness of heart, thinking, "Do we really have to go again?" Frequently, however, God has met me there and proved, once more, that he can transform the mundane with the sparkle of his presence.

Suggested Activities

1. Draw up a list of other "journeys" you take. Select one or two and ask God to help you understand their significance for your relationship with him. Or, better still, do one of them and note what he "says" to you.

2. If there are "journeys" you find threatening or a chore, why not, each time you must make it, ask God specifically to meet you as you go? When your "journey" is over, spend ten minutes or so retracing your steps. Perhaps God's presence was obvious – make some notes about it, perhaps there seems to be nothing special – ask him to show you if you missed anything, like a person to pray for, a poster that made you smile and contained a strange truth, an opportunity to help someone you missed, or someone who was kind to you. Was there a conflict sparked off in your mind, which you failed to note? Perhaps these kinds of issues will alert you to God's moments on your "journeys".

Notes
1. See Michael Schluter and David Lee, *The R Factor* (London, 1993).

12 LOOKING, HEAR, AND THERE!

The visual image dominates our modern Western perception; that is why our eyes matter to us so much and why so much is spent on eye care, but equally why many of us spend so much time on our outward appearance – hair, make-up, clothes.

A couple of days ago, a woman, about to become a grandmother yet again was telling me excitedly of her privilege. She had gone with her daughter (one of three married children) to the hospital. Her daughter was expecting her third child in a fortnight's time and was having her third scan for this baby. Grandmother went too and was ecstatic at the view of this almost fully formed baby which the scan-monitor revealed. She could see the baby with all its features before it was born. Yes, she had been able to make out its form, but also see the heart beating as it pumped blood. If we had a different kind of eyes we could see through body tissue all the time and our world view would be very different, to say the least. We see so much, but equally we miss so much because of the specific limits of our visionary capability. To us it seems our sight gives us the picture of reality; a visit to the pre-natal department of gynaecology suggests otherwise. It gives us only one – a very beautiful and rich perception, but not the whole truth. This awareness itself should give us pause to think about how we view each other and how God views us too. It is a serious encouragement to look beyond surface, shapes, colours, and contours to their realities.

However, the main thrust of this chapter is to help us recognize that God can meet us through our non-visual capacities as well as our visual ones.

Full-blown visions are by no means the norm; they are quite exceptional. Yet Isaiah's account of his vision, through which he is called to be a prophet (Isaiah 6), is powerful and instructive because of the varied components which contribute to it, as well as its message. Clearly and dominantly there was the visual element; but there was much more. There was an audible component, in the cries of the seraphim and presumably noise accompanied the shaking of the threshold. This would also be "felt", as was the touch of the burning coals on Isaiah's lips. Almost certainly there was also a contribution through smell, as the temple was filled with smoke. So even a remarkable vision confirms our suspicion that God can communicate with us through any of our senses.

With this in mind, let me now take you back to one of our early episodes where we learnt to listen to the many sounds we normally block out – to the sounds outside the house, the sounds around us in the room and even the sounds within us (see Chapter 5).

We thought there about how, though often unconsciously, we cut so much out of our registered hearing and of how this suggests we could listen more responsively to God as well as other people.

One of God's cries is that we often do not listen even when we hear; one of God's calls is that his people listen to him attentively.

> *The Almighty God, the Lord, speaks;*
> *he calls to the whole earth from east to west.*
> ...
>
> *"Listen, my people, and I will speak;*
> *I will testify against you, Israel.*
> *I am God, your God."*

Psalms 50.1, 7

In most areas of speciality we can learn "to listen with greater understanding", by which I mean to register sounds around us we normally ignore and, as we listen to the sounds, interpret their significance. One of my boyhood memories is that of waiting on shadowy railway stations hearing the dull clang of metal on metal, sounding like the slowed down beat of a pendulum clock. It was, of course, a railway fitter, tapping each wheel of each coach with his hammer. From the tone of the sound he could discern when a wheel was beginning to crack.

There are far more sophisticated opportunities to learn to listen in our modern world. We have looked at the car engine, but any good mechanic will want to listen to it as well. If you know a competent do-it-yourself mechanic – or better still if you are on good terms with your garage, go along and ask your friend to teach you how to listen to the engine – the purrs, the ticks, the hiccups, the burrs and whirls are all coming from the different parts of the comprehensive process. The fan belt, the valves, the timing chain, the spark plugs, the distributor, the starter motor, the pistons, anything that moves and vibrates will make a noise, and the keen-eared mechanic will be able to listen into the sounds. That is, they will be able to get inside the various sounds, mentally to identify them and compare them with some mysterious standard register, and so discern what is and what is not normal, what is significant in helping to identify the problem or the cause of it. To the uninitiated there is only one noise, to the expert a multiplicity of clear messages.

A similar encounter can be gained through working with an orchestral conductor. Most of us will not have one we can approach personally – the nearest we get is through a "master class" on television. How do they hear which violin is out of step, how do they know which trombone is out of tune? How can they tell that the second flute is not sticking to its score? There are so many instruments in an orchestra contributing to an endearing, stirring, unified sound – broken for me only by the appointed interjection of the percussionist. How anyone can pick out the discordant from the group of instruments, I don't think I will ever know. Yet the conductor can and must, in order to draw the individual into enhancing unity.

We need to learn to listen to the complex sounds and system of sounds around us.

But it is important we train ourselves not only to listen so as to discern our faults and correct them, but also so that we can encourage the good, praise the promising, affirm the valuable. The good mechanic can hear beauty in a well-tuned engine, he or she will know what is right and when the whole mechanical orchestration[1] is running purposefully and properly they will say so, and take pleasure in it. Their task is to restore the right noise when they hear the telling notes of discomfort and damage.

No conductor is going to give birth to creative, imaginative interpretation through the orchestra unless they can engender enthusiasm as well as correct faults. So, one thing God may well say to us – he certainly does to me – is, "listen to your listening". I know I not only need to learn to listen with far greater discernment so that I can distinguish what is this from what is that, instead of dismissing everything as noise, I not only need to learn to listen so that I can identify what the problem may be, I also need to learn to listen to the way I listen, so as not to focus only on what is wrong. I may be able to hear the languages of people and angels, but if I have no love, I will hear no more than a noisy gong or clanging bell. I may have the gift of delicate hearing, I may recognize all sounds and understand all noises... but if I have no love, I am nothing (1 Corinthians 13, adapted!).

There is at least one step more I need to take – to listen to the way I express my awareness when I hear things are wrong.

No more lying, then! Everyone must tell the truth to one another, because we are all members together in the body of Christ. ... Do not use harmful words but only helpful words, the kind that build up and provide what is needed, so that what you say will do good to those who hear you.

Ephesians 4.25, 29. Verses 30–31
are worth reading aloud to ourselves too!

Not all modern sounds are helpful though. A few weeks ago I was staying in a Christian conference centre. I woke in the middle of the night to hear a persistent and irritating metallic sound. My mind started to work on identifying it so that I could stop it and return to sleep. After a few minutes puzzling and grasping my way up to reasonable alertness, I decided it must be the metal coat hangers (the sort you collect free from dry cleaners) swinging in the wooden wardrobe and clinking on the sides. Light on, enter the wardrobe, remove coat hangers, and return to blissful slumber. A few minutes back in the warm and the same noise started again. It must be the coat hanger on the door. Same procedure. But once back in bed, the irritating noise recurred. Eventually I discovered a pattern. Far away in the distance, somewhere, I would hear the central heating system switch on – then the sound. It was in fact the large bore central heating pipes moving on the metallic hoop brackets as they expanded their way round the circumference of my room and then, moments later, started to contract again. What could I do? I wanted to be warm and was grateful for the heat – anyway in the middle of the night I had neither power, nor authority, to summon the heating engineer, nor the knowledge to go and silence the boilers – although I must admit, all such possibilities and many more passed through my mind as I lay there, craving sleep and trying, in vain, to blot out these intrusive sounds from my mind.

Perhaps – no probably – I am like such a noise to some people around me, in some ways. They can't do without me, may not even wish to, but I cause disturbance, tension, and irritation in their lives, particularly at moments when there is nothing and no one else to bother them. I invade their privacy and their peace because of something I have said, for which I have not apologized, because of a character trait, a behaviour pattern. I do not suppose those responsible for my well-being in that conference centre wanted to inflict disturbance on my sleep – but they did. So out of that experience has come a prayer that I might become more sensitive to the inadvertent repercussions of me, of even the good I seek to do and to be; even my helpfulness may turn into "irritating noises" for others.

But I realize too that others may be inflicting similar annoyance on me in the same way. I may not always be aware of what their tone, their gestures, their comments are doing to me, any more than I was aware of the continuing noise of the pipes during the day time. It was only because I was "forced" to listen, that I became conscious of the irritation building up internally. Equally, I need to listen in the silence, maybe even the silence of the sleepless night and seek to identify the cause of tension, frustration, anger, anxiety, etc. My experience that night taught me that my first identification of the problem and its solution was wrong, although I was so delightedly sure that I had peace within my grasp at the first attempt. So, we need to tread cautiously in identifying the source of our problems. It should never be with the intention of accusing others, only of resolving the issue. In the end, the solution to the noisy metal pipes was simple – fold some scrap paper and lodge it between the brackets and the pipe. It was for me to resolve the problem – it may not have looked very beautiful to others who entered my room and noticed my idiosyncratic tendencies! To them it would seem odd, but it was cheap and it was easy; it was within my power with God's help. So through that experience God is speaking to me about my relationships with others and how to ease the problems of which I become aware. As God said to Paul over a far more desperate kind of intrusion and irritation:

My grace is all you need, for my power is greatest when you are weak.

2 Corinthians 12.9

There are other noises which intrude and which are even more appropriate symbols for our modern world. One of the most annoying and insistent is the home burglar alarm which frequently seems to go off, without provocation. So frequent and so annoying is this "false" alarm that government legislation is being drafted to try and curb the problem.

The fact that we need them is a sign of a very unhappy society, where divisions between the haves and have-nots are so powerful, where the significance of owning material things is rated so highly that some will do almost anything to obtain "what does not belong to them" and others will do almost anything to protect "what does belong to them". Burglar alarms represent a warring conflict of social attitudes of what is fair and just, of the right of might, of jealousy, anger, fear, the breakdown of neighbourliness, and many other things. As I hear the burglar alarm resounding through the streets, it is as though I hear the mood of our society, amplified through the anguish of God.

TOUCH

We can "look" through our sense of touch as well. When I left my last church some friends gave me a wooden cross which had been carefully contoured, sanded, polished to hold in the hand as an aid to prayer. I have still to master it – for me it is an object of care and beauty, a gift of love, but I have not learnt to feel prayer flowing through me, prompted by the tactile sensation. For others, such features can be a tremendous help to devotion – praying the rosary is one special illustration. Yet that is not to say I have nothing to experience and learn through my sense of touch.

An hour ago I was wondering what I would have to say to a clinically white piece of paper. I knew the subject of the chapter I would be trying to write, but my mind was almost blank. However, once I took hold of the cheap stick ballpoint pen, the thoughts, the images, the words, the joy of communication began to flow. Holding the pen somehow helps to make the connection for me; it acts like a probe which enters my psyche and releases a flow of mental methane gas from the resources hidden within me. Sometimes I think I should change to typing on a word processor – it would have several advantages – but I am afraid that all my creative energy would be either channelled into concentrating on the keys, or side-streamed off into frustration with the processes. The result would be that I would lose my way. So, I continue with my arm ache and untidiness, with my loss of "editing" facility because a pen between fingers and thumb does the trick! Why?

For me one of the most telling of tactile experiences is that of "shaking hands". Perhaps it has no special place in a book about God at the end of the century because it has nothing technological about it! Yet through this social convenience so much can be experienced and communicated – warmth and welcome, caution and control, fear and openness, strength and frailty. God has much to say about hands, too, and has spoken to us through Christ's hands in many ways.

Some people have hands that seem so capable of discovering their environment. Others are competent in shaping their environment. Here is an aspect of meditation which I am sure I must leave to others to fill out. I remain convinced, however, that for some of us, this will be a penetrating way to discover truths about God and from God.

As Wink says, "The hands have a wisdom the mind does not know".[2]

Perhaps, for those who lack manual dexterity like me, there is the possibility of using hands in role play rather than working with clay. For instance, to share in "a foot washing" service, in which the example of Jesus in John 13 is re-enacted, as happens in some churches on Maundy Thursday may provide powerful experiences of God's loving care and compassion.

Or maybe different "body" experiences will be the way for others to discover God's presence in the world. While some people find "dance in worship" a distraction to watch, and others find it helpful, expressive, and significant, we who watch should also bear in mind its values for those who do it. They do it, not as a performance but as a living expression of the music they are hearing, the words of Scripture that have challenged them or the feelings within them – all offered to God as a worshipful response. In so doing they are affirming that our bodies are God's creation and they are offering their whole selves back to him. As people worship God in dance they can be open to respond to God; through the availability of their bodies God can meet with them, and they can discover insights about joy and pain, relationships, freedom, and restrictions, which can be a vehicle for meditative insight. Of course, such physical expression is not restricted to the public arena; it can be very significant as a form of private devotion. Nor does it have to be whole body movement. I have found insight and understanding as I have lived out the words of a song through simply arm and hand movements. I have also met with God on my knees – as had Paul.

What I am trying to state in this section is that meditation can be through physical expression and body movement, as well as through the more passive kind of meditation using our eyes.

SMELL

Our ability to smell is another form of communication through which God can speak to us in our modern world. Unlike the early hunter we have comparatively little facility with this gift. Yet there are special and sensitive things about smell. There is still the strange, musty smell of rain falling after a long, dry spell. Just this last Saturday, a speaker I heard was saying how a few days earlier he had opened a pot of apricot jam – and that very special sweet deep smell had taken him straight back 40 years to when he was a child of 5 years old and his mother had hidden a pill she was trying to get him to take in a spoonful of apricot jam. I wanted to leap up and interrupt the speaker, and discover from him what thoughts and feelings were captured which the smell of apricot jam released. Did he feel deceived and cheated by his mother? Or did he sense a loving kindness from her? How did he view it now? I could have had a fascinating time, but it had to slip away. With smell that is often what happens – we let it slip away.

Because the associations of smell are so fragile and so easily evaporate from our mental awareness, we need to note them with great alertness and eagerness. Yet even this, it seems to me, can, as it were, frighten them away, like trying to capture a butterfly.

Scripture and song also know of the evocative power of smell. There is a beautiful song which captures something very special about Jesus:

> *May the fragrance of Jesus fill this place*
> *Lovely fragrance of Jesus*
> *Rising from the sacrifice*
> *Of lives laid down in adoration.* [3]

Perfume can be the distinctive indicator of a loved one. Although without visual identification, the familiar scent evokes an image, or even their presence, and somehow, at times, even more powerfully than their picture, or even their visible presence would.

So, Jesus is like a delicate perfume, announcing that someone wonderful is nearby. It seems to me a very appropriate metaphor for "him whom my soul loves".

Jesus talked about the smell of perfume being a testimony for all time of the loving generosity of a woman (Mark 14.3–9). Paul picks on a similar metaphor but with a much more bitter flavour.

> *But thanks be to God! For in union with Christ we are always led by God as prisoners in Christ's victory procession. God uses us to make the knowledge about Christ spread everywhere like a sweet fragrance. For we are like a sweet-smelling incense offered by Christ to God, which spreads among those who are being saved and those*

who are being lost. For those who are being lost, it is a deadly stench that kills; but for those who are being saved, it is a fragrance that brings life. Who, then, is capable of such a task?

2 Corinthians 2.14–16

Here is the picture of captured slaves, filthy, brutalized, bleeding – on their way to slaughter as part of the celebration of some great general's victory. The subject of Paul's meditation was very contemporary and not the least restful, romantic, or natural.

How can smell bring us into touch with God's reality?

Today we can capture "smells" in a can – so we use sprays to "freshen" the air. In a way we are choosing to be courteous and thoughtful. Such synthetic "fragrance" has its place in modern society. There are times when God calls us to act in a similar way, by providing a kind diversion to help people avoid a damaging argument, or by affirming positive words to help someone through a personal crisis. Here is a challenge from God, but also a warning that I should not become a cover-up for my own unpleasantness.

Sometimes smells help to create our appetite. It is often the case that the meal being prepared can smell better than it tastes. Anyway what we think of as taste is largely smell (or so my scientific son tells me). Certainly we eat often because of the smell, rather than because we are deliberately taking in the required quantities of vitamins, proteins, carbohydrates, etc. Here is a message from God. Perhaps he does not worry too much about why we (and others) want to meet him and belong to him. Maybe our theology does not have to be correct before we can benefit from our relationship with him. God makes himself attractive to allure us.

Not all smells are attractive and that, too, often has value. The absence of "smell" in natural gas can be a problem – so an unpleasant "smell" is added in order that we are alert to the dangers. Sometimes dangerous gases can not be smelt. We think we have an adequate warning system through our sense of smell, but it is not adequate for the potential dangers of our modern world. Perhaps God has something to say to us through this as well. Perhaps Christians need to insert the warning into activities and attitudes so that others keep away from the dangers.

I am well aware that such reflections seem rather "wooden" and lacking in the directness of the more mental and imaginative meditations with which I am most comfortable. That is because of the way I operate. But I wanted to include some hints as to how touch and smell might be useful as a form of meditation, because I know that other people will have far greater "success" in hearing God through these faculties. I very much want to encourage people to be open to these possiblities, however hard I find it myself.

I also look towards the day when these aspects of my being will be as alert to God as others.

Suggested Activities

1. In order to assist social workers understand how best to help blind people, they spend a day blindfolded. How would you react to this, do you think? How dependent are we on sight for our view of the world? If possible, spend time with a blind person discovering their view of the world.

2. Why not have a special "listening day"? Ask God to open your ears to hear with understanding. It may help to have a book in which to note "special" sounds you hear. It may be that you deliberately take five minutes here and there to listen to everything you can hear, and to listen to your responses to the various sounds. It may be that you silence your tongue and concentrate on listening more to the other person. All of this can be interlaced with prayer!

3. How do you listen to people? Do you listen to friends in a different way to family members? How well do you listen to people who irritate you – is there a way beyond the barbed wire of irritation to audibly hold the person in love? Do you listen with one ear on "What can I say?" or do you listen, and make listening the whole task? When you have learnt to listen, can you go on to hear what God is saying through the human listening?

4. How important are smell and touch to you? Have you ever offered them to God as a part of the whole self we are to consecrate to him? (Romans 12.1–3)

Notes

1. Perhaps you sense this to be an awkward word in view of the parallel metaphor. However, I have chosen it deliberately – to the mechanic the engine running well is "music"! There is value in sensing connections between different "worlds" – we may find God more easily in one than the other but both can be accessible to God.

2. *Transforming Bible Study*, p.120.

3   Graham Kendrick, *Songs of Fellowship* (Kingsway Music, 1991).

13 LOOKING NOW

One of the marks of our modern society is "rush". Everything has to happen now, this instant. We must hurry through every experience lest we miss the next and in so doing we do not take to ourselves this moment, here and now, with all its strength and delicacy. Any book which is meant to help with meditating in our modern world must take seriously the fact that computers perform billions of operations per second and the research is in place to speed this up beyond my powers to enumerate.

Computers are not alone in working at speed. Human beings also perform high speed operations but they are not the ones which seem pertinent to us. An advertisement told me just how many muscles I moved while walking past the poster – I don't remember and I don't care very much, and it certainly does not encourage me to join that medical scheme. For such factors are not where I sense the source of my life to be, even if my life depends on it. Yet our life does run very fast. For many of us, it is moments and minutes, not hours and days, which will be the opportunity to grow into our awareness of God with us and so develop our relationship with the God who dwells in eternity. This relationship is one we need even more if we are to survive the present hectic pace. Few people refuse the offer of a mobile phone. It means that contact with those you love can be snatched to help sustain, although not to be a substitute for, those longer times of intimacy which such relationships warrant. In the same way we can discover our special opportunities, our moments of communication, in the headlong rush between getting up and going to sleep, which can help us maintain our relationship with God.

Before we seek to identify those times in our lives and see how we can best seize them it is helpful to consider all the dimensions of meditation we have covered. We will then relate these different kinds of meditation to our briefer opportunities.

In Chapter 7 (Looking Around) we began to take more careful notice of the objects and situations which make up much of our modern world. Although a great deal of "our world" is a manufactured environment rather than a "natural" one, we soon discovered that our world is also one through which God can speak to us. This is an important and significant understanding to reach because it opens up a multiplicity of opportunities for our encounters with God. To rule it out is like refusing ever to listen to someone on the telephone on the grounds that it is "not natural" or "not real". In practice most of us know the telephone works very well, although this does not mean it is best for every kind of communication. Equally, in seeking to establish that our synthetic world has great potential and validity as a medium for meditation, we are not claiming it is the best, or mocking the more usual focuses for meditation; rather we are seeking to explore its possibilities and, inevitably, also its limits for each one of us.

From here on we began to explore our world in more specific ways. Looking inwards helped us examine the intricacies of things around us that we might never normally bother with; this may be because we have no need to do so or may be because we consider we lack the necessary competence to look into things. Both of these views are themselves reflections on our modern world. Breaking out of these strait-jackets may itself create new possibilities for us to meet with God. The former (i.e. we have no need) emphasizes the utilitarian ethos – "If it's not useful it must be a waste of time". It is not easy to see what use "meditation" is, but then is it not necessary to justify everything human beings do on utilitarian grounds? God made us for himself; it is true, our hearts are restless until we rest in him. We need to consider the purpose for which we are made before we can begin to assess whether it is a good thing we are doing. The latter (i.e. the perceived lack of competence) emphasizes the world of experts and the inevitable segregation that this generates. If experts remain isolated they can easily become dangerous. It is very easy for their subjects and the pursuit of their potential, to become ends in themselves: the results of such micromania have caused untold damage. Meditating on things we do not fully understand will not save us from such tunnel vision but we do not need to be frightened off from looking into the worlds which fascinate others, on the grounds that it is forbidden territory. So we looked at the "engine" of a car and the structure of an electrical plug.

Looking Backwards (Chapter 9) was an opportunity to bring another human dimension into our approach to meditation; for we are more than cameras registering what is before our eyes. Perception is an interactive process. So, in this section, we deliberately freed up our memories and allowed all kinds of experiences from our past to flow towards us, triggered by the object on which we focused. This works rather like a powerful magnet attracting all kinds of metal objects towards it until they cluster on top of one another. Having collected them haphazardly, we can arrange the objects in some kind of order if we so choose. So it is with our memories; they come from varied depths, they come in all shapes and sizes, they collect themselves at untidy angles to the magnetic force. Yet through them God may show us many truths and lead us to opportunities of delight or healing. This process normally brings to us a greater sense of integration and well-being, although such a sense may take time to reach.

Looking Outwards (Chapter 10) took us along a completely different pathway. Here we allowed the materials from which very ordinary, everyday objects had been manufactured to direct the process. They led us into other countries of the world and situations we would rarely think about. Ordinary materials acted as windows through which we could look, or doors we could open and travel through into worlds that are new to us, and yet worlds which impact on us. In doing this we are taking the first steps in turning contingent (depersonalized) relationships into contact (more properly human) relationships and so we make a small contribution to investing our world with personhood again.

In the Looking Away chapter (Chapter 11) we recognized that much of our contemporary experience is not so much about "standing and staring" as about "going and doing". We found that many of the activities which fill our busy, mundane lives can also become channels for divine challenge. They actually contain experiences (although like modern medicine they may be foil-wrapped and gelatine-encapsulated so we don't know what we are taking – least of all what they taste like) which probe us and our value systems, and thus provide God with opportunities to show us who we are, and what we may be in danger of becoming. They can act like mirrors and help us see where our lives need straightening out, correcting, readjusting – although before this confrontation with ourselves takes place we may need to demist the mirror of our complex modern experiences. Often this can be done by more reflection on what is going on in our lives. Sometimes the light of insight will shine on us through a complementary process such as reading a book, or hearing someone's comment. This can be like a laser beam which penetrates where light normally will not reach. In this way also we are hearing God call us to himself and to ourselves. Such experiences are very much part of the value of traditional meditation, giving us as they do a chance to reorientate ourselves and start off again with greater confidence and enthusiasm, sensing we are now travelling in the right direction.

Chapter 12, Looking, Hear, and There, was a brief reminder that we are not only blessed with the gift of sight, but with hearing, touch, taste, and smell as well. Each of these is a gift from God which can link us with our world in such a way that he meets with us. Yesterday I heard a sermon about the Magi. It was full of helpful insights; not least that many saw the same night sky but only the Magi saw its significance and ended up meeting God. That is exactly what we are trying to learn to do with all our senses; to move beyond the surface, and so be led to meet with God and worship him who made the world.

There is no reason at all why these different approaches should be kept in separate boxes. They can also be mixed and matched as we choose, as our minds select, or as God appoints. We can listen to the cornflake box, feel it, allow it to generate memories, explore the intricacies of its design etc. When we visit the dentist our other senses will be bombarded into life and they can be given freedom to dominate our meditative process etc. I hope everyone is clear that the different aspects have received differentiated attention in order to develop facility in them all. But they belong together as the situation requires. It is like learning how to drive a car. Different aspects of driving will receive attention in different lessons, but ultimately they are all necessary and need to come together in the right combinations for progress, manoeuvrability, and safety.

So, what we have now is a considerable range of approaches to our modern world which, separately or together, provide us with resources for meeting with God in our world today and any day. We have, if you wish to picture it this way, a cupboard full of ingredients we can call on. But sometimes we must get our meal together very quickly – or not bother eating, because we don't have the time.

In the second half of this chapter, therefore, I want to encourage us to bother with our moments. Not every meditative meal needs to be a gourmet one. We sometimes need to be sustained on the run. This does not mean we should not seek for longer times of reflection or, indeed, of retreat. But we are not isolated from God when such opportunities are not available. So let us consider when and how we may seize our moments for God.

SEIZING OUR MOMENTS

In each life there are a multiplicity of moments that can be used for meditation. With some awareness and practice these moments can be discovered and become very fruitful. The moments will be different for each of us, and not all I list are likely to be available to any one person, but almost certainly as you consider your own day you will discover many, many more you could utilize.

Here are some of them that come to my mind from my experience. There is the moment, several times a day, when I come to put a key in the lock – in fact this is not one moment but several. There is thinking where the key is and then trying to find it in innumerable pockets (why are the keys invariably in the last pocket I dig into?), there is fitting the key (hopefully the right one) into the lock, there is the moment of success, turning the lock, opening the door, taking the key out, and trying to note in my mind for later which pocket I have put it in.

There are moments with the telephone – dialling moments, tone moments, transfer moments.

There are varied moments with the television, such as moments when we walk in and out of a room, and we see only a small squint from a long programme. There are the deliberate moments of the soap-style presentation when, although we may watch the whole programme, every 30 seconds or so we are whisked to a different situation. There are moments of advertisements.

There are waiting moments. These come in many shades and shapes but are similar in some ways. There is waiting for a train – or even waiting at the barrier to have a ticket checked. There is waiting for stamps at the post office, waiting in the car for the traffic lights to change or the car in front (sorry, large, articulated lorry, so it often seems) to move. There are longer times too – regularly on tube trains, less frequently in doctors' waiting rooms, and similar situations.

There are moments when we wait for things to operate. The times we stand in the lift and press the button – the doors must close and then we journey upwards. Or there is the pause when we return home on a dark night and first enter our home with a sense both of familiarity and apprehension. We press the switch and wait a few endless seconds for the fluorescent tube to flicker, glow, and then steadily illuminate the dark scene. There are the moments – again, often only a few seconds –

before the stereo, computer, or television are operational, moments for the iron to heat up, or the kettle to boil. All can become God opportunities.

There are also many situations where we can be doing something but our whole being is not fully occupied – nor does it need to be. Those occasions when we are "filling" the car with petrol, "doing" the washing up, hanging out the recently washed clothes, stirring the soup or holding the hand whisk, shaving, drying our hair, etc.

All of these moments have the potential to become occasions when we can feed our spirits by making them times for God. So let us look a little more carefully at the opportunities we have here. But before we do here is a word of caution, which is meant primarily to be a word to encourage.

I have emphasized that within every busy person's day there are many brief moments which we can claim for, and offer to, God. I suspect there will be dozens in even the most frenetic day. Not only will the content of each list vary from person to person, so also will the degree of feasibility for grasping any kind of time for God. One person may sense that the washing up is an ideal time, another will not because pain caused by arthritis dominates their awareness at such moments. One will favour the lift, while another will be panicking at the thought of entombment within it. Some people will be glad to invite God into their car while they are waiting at the traffic lights, for another this occasion will not seem at all conducive to meditation, only heightened frustration. Where is it best to make a start? Please start this developmental process with those short situations which seem possible, with those where your response is – "Oh, what a good idea, I can't wait to try it. Why didn't I think of that?" – and not those which seem impossible or ultra difficult to you and where you groan inwardly, "The man must be crazy, I struggle to cope anyway, I can't add that burden to my list". Obviously if we start with the "no go" areas we will conclude that the whole approach is impossible. If we start with those which really seem opportune, then like ripe apples which are hanging waiting to be plucked as we go by, we are more likely to succeed, than if we seek to handle the difficult ones. In fact, washing up for the arthritic, and lift moments for the panicking, can become times with God of great value, but they are almost certainly not the place to begin. So please be very selective with what follows. Hopefully, there will be at least one section which feels comfortable for you, which you can identify by comparing with your own list of "good" opportunities.

KEYS

Keys represent for me a sense of privilege. I suppose that goes with the old saying "the key to the door", implying for the 21 year old they now had sufficient maturity to be allowed to come in when they decided and not when parents dictated; they no longer had to be given permission to come in later than normal; it was no longer a special and gracious dispensation, it was their right. Each key I carry represents a different privilege. The key to the car – the freedom of mobility, to travel in comfort, and if not with ease, at least without getting out of breath. It is the key to visiting friends, to exploring new places, and returning to well-loved haunts. It is a key which bridges work and leisure. For me the car is an essential tool to get around the country to speaking engagements as well as to meetings for planning and consultation. Yet it is also the key to holidays and family occasions. Both, in different ways, are sources of satisfaction and enjoyment. So it is highly appropriate that one key signifies both. The car is a place of privacy – on some busy days it may be the only space I have; time for reflecting, for praying, for preparation; time even to listen to music, catch up on the current news, or brush up on a language ready for travel abroad. However, the car is also a place of companionship – as I may travel with others, friends, or members of the family. Here are many avenues of prayer – some tree-lined and magnificent, running for miles into my past and on into the future, prompting flowing thanks and deep gratitude. Others are small culs-de-sacs – a brief journey shared. Not only thanks but intercession can be prompted by this key – for those I have shared a journey with, for those to whom I travel etc., so that key, reminding me of the privilege of the car, brings a million raindrops for prayer, which water my life. Only one or two may fall on me each time I use that key, but what a privilege.

The other even more significant key is the key to my home. Again there are many notches on this Yale key. In some ways my key is very similar to hundreds of other home owners, but I know that my key is quite distinctive. That distinctiveness reminds me, in a second, of the similarity of my family to many others, but also of the particularity of my wife, my two sons, and my daughter. I can thank God for their variety; for their uniqueness. But the key to my home is a series of notches arranged in a specific order. So we as a family belong together and for us to function properly we need to stay in proper and positive relationships with each other. Here is another dimension to my prayers. I also recall that each member of the family has a key just like mine. We all have the privilege of entrance into that home; it is not mine, it is ours – sometimes that leads to confession as I reflect on my selfishness. My key sticks in the lock – it doesn't slide in smoothly and release the latch straight away. Here, too, is a message for my prayers that we may live, work, and grow harmoniously; occasionally there will be a very pressing and specific issue which requires prayer along these lines. The very fact that we need a lock that always locks rather than a mortice lock which we only close at night, is another focus. For homes now need more security than before, because of the many and frequent dangers from intruders. The parallel with the home and family life is not hard to see. Again, this aspect of the key to my home is an instant prompt to prayer.

On my key ring is also a key to the church of which I am a member and at which I was one of its full-time paid ministers for twelve years. Holding that key is a very special privilege and walking through that door leads to a myriad of opportunities for prayer, as all will easily imagine.

Another key is the key to the Automobile Association phone boxes, reminding me of the value of emergency services when I break down. The connections with God are obvious. So, for me, it is important that the emergency key is an indication of belonging to an organization which does much more than provide emergency help when the car breaks down. I am provided with maps and a gazetteer – have I consulted the Bible properly today? It is an organization which has sought to change with changing times, so is the Evangelical Alliance for which I now work; both are groups of people seeking to work together for mutual benefit. Belonging to both is a privilege.

So here are four of the many keys on my key ring; each prompts prayer which leaps forth from the sense of privilege with which they are connected. Obviously, covering all these aspects in the minute or less between finding the key and using it itself takes weeks. Each person's keys will lead them in many directions, some similar to mine maybe but others completely personal to them. Please may I encourage you to listen to God through your keys.

The perceptive reader will have sensed that my keys are quite numerous and therefore weighty in my pocket. Besides privilege, keys represent for me responsibility. They also remind me of others who carry even heavier responsibilities. I think of the duty manager in a large hotel, of people who run risks as security patrollers, of police officers who seek to preserve order and fairness, of prison officers who have the unenviable responsibility of locking people up and depriving them of their freedom. So my keys, besides reminding me to pray about my responsibilities, to pray for clarity of perception, reliability, a servant heart and so forth, also call me to pray for others in positions of responsibility.

Another point which comes to me through my keys is almost incidental. Somehow as they lay in my pocket they sometimes manage to intertwine themselves. So, like some ferocious Chinese puzzle, before I can use the one I require, I have to disentangle them from each other. Is it only my keys that do this, I wonder? However, this frustrating experience (especially when I am in a hurry) underlines for me the fact that my keys, representing different features of my life, can also, like those areas of life, get in a tangle. Priorities are not always easily kept in order. Here too is an issue for prayer, reminding me that if they are not kept in their proper place none of them is any use.

It is not only when I come to use my keys that they prompt me to pray. Sometimes through the day I will feel their edges on my leg. Sometimes as I hurry from one task to another I will hear them. Other senses too come into play and momentarily activate my mind and spirit in a God-ward direction.

THE LIFT

There are three distinct opportunities for prayer associated with lifts. The first is waiting for the lift to arrive. Occasionally (and why is it so occasionally?) there is the unexpected joy of the lift actually being there waiting for me, instead of me having to wait for it! This very special and rare experience prompts me to thank God for the very special (and in my experience more frequent) times when I sense he has arranged for a significant encounter or chain of events, so that issues which could have taken hours of hard work to sort out simply fall into place. Normally, however, there is the process of waiting for the lift! The button is pushed to summon the lift (I have to confess often three times, even though I know it will not cause the lift to come any quicker) and then all I can do is wait. There are at least two ways this prompts me to reflect prayerfully. The first is the simple recognition that I am living through a parable on prayer itself. I have called to God and he has promised to answer, but I don't like waiting. Waiting for the lift underlines this fact. Often I also have a choice – do I climb the stairs or do I wait for the lift? Many things can be done on my own – but not all. Should I wait for God to answer my prayers? Is doing it myself (climbing the stairs) disobedience, foolhardiness, the long way round, or is that what God wants me to do?

Then, waiting for the lift reminds me of other lifts I have waited for. In hospitals to visit dying patients, as well as to see my wife and new-born child. Lifts in blocks of flats, with all kinds of encounters to follow. Lifts in shops, in car parks, in hotels, as well as where I now find myself most usually waiting, at an underground station lift. Any one of these situations can fill my (hopefully!) brief duration waiting for the lift, by bringing me into touch with God.

Further opportunities for prayer, as far as lifts are concerned, are the times of anticipation. The floor indicator, or the whirring, clattering noises tell me the lift is on the way; the doors open and the occupants disgorge themselves and now I am the lucky one; the internal "door close" button is pushed and I am anticipating my arrival some time soon at my destination. Two focuses for prayer are prevalent during this stage of the journey. First, there is the obvious issue of anticipation. I can bring to God the features of my life labelled that way. There are the immediate purposes of my using the lift; the people I am hoping to meet, the problems I expect to have to resolve, the plans I am preparing to make, the decisions I need to reach, the actions that must be performed. Each of these warrants a prayerful moment. But I can also pray for others I know of who are living in a state of anticipation – driving tests, babies, exam results, appointments, operations, unemployment, death. All kinds of situations and people have flashing over them "anticipation". Sometimes a door which repeatedly fails to close, or a lift which stops at every floor, and may even decide to go down again before I arrive at my exit level, is an additionally valuable cue, underlining the needs and emotions which are generated when anticipation is not fulfilled as expected!

The waiting stage also causes me to focus on the people with whom I share the lift. Normally I don't know them, although if we share a lift in a block of flats or to reach our work station, we may know some of them. Either situation is an opportunity to pray for them, to allow the love God has for all to flow through us, to earnestly desire God's blessing on them. Here is a unique constellation of human life; we may never be able to pray for just this group again. On occasions some specific needs will be obvious

– an old person struggling even to get into the lift, a foreign visitor with an underground map or phrase book in their hand, a mechanic or plumber with their toolbag. Then we can be more specific in our moment's prayer. Sometimes, too, we may, under the direction of the Holy Spirit, or through our own perceptions, sense special issues for prayer. In our minds we can seek to link the person with God.

Finally, as far as lifts are concerned, we have an opportunity for prayer as the lift ascends or descends. Usually my first prayer is "I hope we arrive soon". Once, just once, I was stuck between floors with a woman and a nine-month-old baby for 45 minutes. It was a small lift, capable of carrying a maximum of only six people, which meant there was hardly room to sit on the floor, and certainly not room for the baby to crawl around, or for me to get away from the noise of the baby's crying. It was a lift without a telephone or other means of signalling for help. The only thing for it, once we realized we were well and truly stuck was to shout for help. It was summer and lifts stuck in shafts can get very hot. It was not an experience I desire to repeat too often. Hence my prayer.

Yet my prayer is not only for myself, but for others who may be far more prone towards claustrophobia than I am. It also leads me on to think of very different circumstances where people feel trapped and from which they can see no escape. There are people in marriages which bring pain and tension, not pleasure and support, those caring for elderly parents, or demanding and disabled children, people trapped in poverty from which, in spite of expending enormous energy, ingenuity and courage, they cannot escape. There are others imprisoned by work, because of the boss they can't cope with, practices which are imposed on them which cut into their consciences, or pressures which crush them because they feel incompetent and inadequate. There are people who are imprisoned by serious disability or terminal illness, others by the haunting of abuse experiences they have endured. There are people "in prison" and the imprisonment this brings their families. Internationally there are horrific war-torn cities from which there is no escape. The list is endless. Once in the lift, you will understand that I am soon wondering "Where is the phone?" Is there some way of seeking help should the worst happen? This reminds me of God's promise that with every testing situation he will provide an escape route. I remember some of the many times I have experienced the powerful truth of that promise. I pray with faith and hope for some who feel trapped.

But back to my "trapped" experience. We were eventually rescued, after many shouts and waits. The lift was hand cranked down to where we started! Normally, however, we arrive safely at our intended destination without such interruptions. Here too is cause for thanksgiving – for the people who service the lift and for all the others, known and unknown, who enable our lives to run smoothly and help us accomplish our purposes. Such a moment is also one for recalling the Scripture:

> *As for me, the hour has come for me to be sacrificed;*
> *the time is here for me to leave this life. I have done my*
> *best in the race, I have run the full distance, and I have*
> *kept the faith. And now there is waiting for me the*
> *victory prize of being put right with God, which the Lord,*
> *the righteous Judge, will give me on that Day – and not*
> *only to me, but to all those who wait with love for him*
> *to appear.*

2 Timothy 4.6–8

The release from the lift is an occasion for giving thanks for those who have arrived at their ultimate destination; a moment to pray for all those who have no idea what their destination is meant to be, or even that there is a destination. And often as I see people leaving the lift and taking a few moments to gain their bearings and work out where to go next, I recall people whose life situation is mirrored in those around me, and pray that they may quickly regain their equilibrium and move smoothly onwards into God's plan.

Each and every moment we are given, each microspace or longer, provides us with time to be with God. In the two instances of keys and lifts I have indicated ways in which the features of the situation can be useful in stimulating us to pray in fairly specific ways. Clearly there are many other types of moments in our lives which can become similar opportunities. It is probably helpful to compile our own list. Many people who have not learnt to practise this kind of meditation think that they don't have them! So to start with, even compiling a list seems a daunting task, but it is an important one.

Opportunity	Frequency	Possible Prayer Dimensions
1. Using keys	8 times a day	1. Privileges 2. Responsibilities 3. Confusion
2. Lifts	4 times a week	1. Anticipation 2. Waiting 3. Arrival
3.		
4.		
5.		

Above I have started my list and you may start yours in a similar way, or perhaps it will be quite different. Obviously from comments I made earlier in this chapter I could add in (3) using the telephone, (4) getting petrol, (5) watching television advertisements, (6) queuing etc. You may well find it helpful to compile your own list – either give yourself half-an-hour, or be prepared to keep coming back to add to your list as you become more and more aware of opportunities. Initially write down the possibilities, then start to calculate the frequency. Finally, either as you reflect on the opportunities, or as you experience them, fill in the third column. Naturally we can go on adding to this column for the rest of our lives.

Making such a list is important because it helps us break out of the confines into which life's rush seems to imprison us. However there are a few further but very important points I wish to make about this kind of process, and particularly the way that I have described it.

First, I am very conscious that as I have described meditations using keys or lifts, it sounds as though all the initiatives for prayer have been my ideas. Where, people might well ask, is God in all of this – wasn't meditation supposed to help us hear God in our world? Now, even if the process was like that, I would want to maintain it was valid and a very beneficial use of time. In a myriad ways I am learning to pray in response to my immediate environment. However the reality is, I believe, rather different, and much more reciprocal. Many of the prayer directions I have suggested come as a result of my being open to God with keys in my hand or waiting for the lift. I now have them at my disposal, but only because God spoke to me, prompted me, showed me possibilities. The descriptions are rather like writing history, but I arrived at them as part of a living relationship with God. This is what makes the whole process so exciting and real. So, if you choose, by all means start off along the lines I have indicated, but you and God are free to say whatever you both choose!

Second, my experience is that almost every time I use the keys or wait for the lift there will be something specific about the experience. The danger in the kind of account I have given is not only that it may suggest all of these thoughts flow through my mind each time I use a key or a lift, but also that that it highlights the recurring features. Yet we all know relationships thrive on the non-recurring. So please be free to be side-tracked and diverted by a raindrop falling on your nose as you put the key in the door, or by the problem of the key getting stuck, or the surprise that the door wasn't locked anyway – or whatever. Here, too, is a wonderful dimension to this kind of prayer moment that almost by definition I cannot prepare people for. All I can do is alert people and say, "God is here". The converse of this is that if people do not become alive to the possibility of meeting God along the general lines I have indicated they are unlikely to be aware of his coming to them in the particularities – their radios will not be switched on in the first place, so to speak.

There is a further consideration to add in to the whole picture. We can deepen and extend the value of these momentary meditations by considering them later at a more leisurely rate. This can partly be achieved along the kind of lines we have been proceeding – each of us can think through and write about opportunities which occur frequently. However, it is possible to gain insight from Scripture as well. Although keys are very much part of our modern way of life they are also a scriptural issue. Any concordance or topical index will soon reveal such insights as we find verses in which the word occurs. That is fairly easy. But how can we proceed when the focus is something modern like lifts? One way is to investigate what Scripture has to teach us about the various matters that lifts bring to mind, for instance "anticipation". Now few modern concordances, let alone those based on the King James (Authorized) Version will reveal much under "anticipation", so the studies have to be more subtle – but there are many passages of Scripture relevant to the theme of anticipation. Some are to do with fairly ordinary matters like birth and harvest. Some are warning us not to "count our chickens before they hatch". Others are to do with macro issues like the return of Jesus.

Equally we can consider "the lift" in the light of Scripture. The lift helps us do what is hard for us alone. In some instances, e.g. the upper stage of the Eiffel Tower, it takes us to places we cannot get without it. Hence we could study the biblical subject of God's grace, or salvation through faith in Christ alone and choose "the lift" as our symbol for these profound realities. Then, whenever we are waiting for the lift we can be transposed into the refreshment of God's ways with us. This is a much more deliberate process than the other approaches, but is equally valid.

What about the person for whom the lift is a threat? In this case I suggest that promises of God are claimed and recalled. There are certainly times when I need to do this too, so that the lift causes us to focus all our attention on God. In this way our spiritual maturity can be enhanced.

So, if we want to use a concordance to help our appreciation of a modern subject for meditation it is worth considering the following steps.

---

1. Write down a list of all the ideas and thoughts associated with your subject. Check which of these are listed in your concordance – these you can consult directly.

2. For those which are not, you can think of Bible passages or themes they call to mind. If you then find those passages you will find which words and concepts are used in the Bible in dealing with them and you can return to your concordance. If your Bible has a chain reference as well, this will help enormously.

3. You may also find that an English thesaurus will give you alternative words to check in your concordance.

4. You may also want to note your responses to this subject of meditation and then you can proceed as with 1 to 3.

However we proceed, it is important that our Bible study is integrated with our meditative processes. It is not the amount of study we do, but its integration which is important.

SUMMARY

In this chapter then we have acknowledged that for many our modern life is a very rushed, pressurized kind of living. However, recognizing that this is a prevailing feature of life at the end of the century, promotes an appropriate kind of meditation which takes this into account.

Somewhat surprisingly we have found that there are several moments in each day – brief moments, it is true, but moments nevertheless – when our lives can be in touch with the living God. Such moments can become special moments of relaxation and spiritual renewal, instead of wasted or frustrating ones. They can be moments of prayer, but also, like seeds, given time to grow, can produce a rich and satisfying harvest.

Developing this kind of spontaneous, frequent but brief encounter with God is enormously refreshing. However, initially, when we are learning the process, it can seem draining – an extra thing to cram into our over-busy schedule. Nevertheless it is worth persevering because, once we have gained the facility we need, it will enrich our relationship with God significantly, not to mention the impact on the world of prayer and intercession which it will generate. We can all find that God is really there for us, whatever speed we move at and however pressurized our pace of life.

14 ENRICHING OUR FAITH

BACK TO WORSHIP

The whole purpose of this book has been to help us become more alert to the presence of God in our everyday world. We have seen that the Bible consistently bears witness to the fact that God is no absentee landlord but "a very present help". He has made the heavens and the earth, and he has walked the earth through Christ. He has not left himself without witnesses within his creation. Anything and anywhere contains the possibility that the ordinary world will quietly and unobtrusively, or maybe even with a shout, declare his glory; that is make his nature and presence clear to us. Furthermore, the Bible indicates that God communicates in a yet more personal fashion within the ordinary places where people work and live, as well as in the special holy places and on especially holy occasions.

To this extent we value the recent emphasis within Western Christian spirituality on meditation, as long as it is distinctively Christian Meditation, which seeks to focus on God's reality and fill our awareness with him, rather than make ourselves empty vessels. Many people have been helped to become more aware of God through meditating on quiet and beautiful realities, such as candles or driftwood, flowers, trees, and water. This is valid and helpful. Many of us need such focuses to help us become aware not only that there is some kind of universal background noise from God, so to speak, but also that he speaks in very personal, and sometimes very precise, ways, through an openness to his presence around us. This is a very important way to learn to hear and see God again.

However, we have discovered that God can meet us just as easily through objects and experiences that are more representative of our contemporary world. Our world is a world of noise, technology, rubbish, and synthetic materials as well as smells. It is a world which moves at a manic pace. Yet this world can also be a world in which speaks God to us. We can certainly be helped by a weekend on retreat in a quiet centre set in rural England, and I would encourage those who can to make use of such opportunities, but we can also be helped to know what God is saying to us while we dial a business number on the phone. This, at least, is the conviction which undergirds this book. If Jesus could discover God in his ordinary, busy, secular world why shouldn't we be able to in ours?

But Jesus did not therefore neglect the ordinary places of worship. He was normally found in the synagogues for worship; he visited the temple and he took part in the religious festivals. Passover seems to be a case in point. Although theologians may dispute the exact details, there is little doubt that when Jesus instituted "the Lord's Supper" he was utilizing aspects of the Passover meal. Yet there is also a sense in which this very sacred service is filled out with (not diminished by) the ordinary everyday world of eating.

While the developmental details may be disputed, Paul's reference to "every time you eat this bread and drink from this cup" (1 Corinthians 11.26), together with the background context of a general meal, added to Luke's comments concerning the early Church, bring together in a fuzzy way the everyday meal and the sacramental meal:

> *They spent their time in learning from the apostles, taking part in the fellowship, and sharing in the fellowship meals and the prayers. ... Day after day they met as a group in the Temple, and they had their meals together in their homes, eating with glad and humble hearts.*

Acts 2.42, 46

So we see each kind of meal enhances the other, and there is a symbiotic relationship – God is present at "ordinary" meals because Christians meet in fellowship. The Lord's Supper is preceded by, or is it incorporated within, an ordinary meal at which the selfish behaviour and immorality of the Corinthians is seriously detrimental to their involvement in the Lord's Supper.

Similarly, we can consider ways in which our awareness of God in our ordinary world can enrich our times of worship. I think there is a parallel between our general state of mind and our involvement in worship which may help us see our extra possibilities. If we go to church and we are feeling particularly tired or unwell it is unlikely (although possible) that we shall hear God, receive his challenge, or experience him in a more intimate way as clearly and effectively as if we go feeling fully alert and full of the joys of spring! Equally, if we go very sensitized because we have entered into a very exciting and loving human relationship, we are likely to become more aware of God's presence in the service of worship. Through that human relationship we may well be "freed up" for unusual levels of self-giving and acts of sacrificial service to the one we love. Within the worship service if we hear God's call on our lives, whether temporary or more long term, we may be "freed up" to respond in an unusually disinterested and courageous way.

I want to encourage us then to take all the skills and sensitivities which we have been developing from our modern world into our more religious activities. We have learnt the value of relaxing – divesting ourselves of tensions which may be unhelpful for fully hearing what is going on around us. We can use this, too, to prepare us for worship in more formal contexts – breathing more slowly and more deeply – relaxing our bodies and our minds may enhance our availability for God. Our experience that there are many ordinary sounds we are missing normally which we can learn to hear, may heighten our expectation that God may also be saying things we don't normally hear. This heightened expectation may enable us to receive much more, both qualitatively and quantitatively.

We are all surrounded in our place of worship by objects which have religious significance. The number and impact of such objects will vary from tradition to tradition. Catholic and Orthodox traditions will provide many more than a House Church or the Society of Friends, but there are some there for all of us. We can use our now more developed abilities to explore and investigate these. We can, for instance, utilize our "backwards look", giving a richer dimension to our perceptions and our resonance with these objects as we recall our personal memories, but also the community's memories of these objects. We may know, or may wish to discover, how they came to be where they are, who gave them, and why. We may recall times when the particular objects were, or are, especially in the limelight for some acts of worship. To some extent we all exercise these abilities I think. It is hard for someone who has been baptized as a believer not to recall their own baptismal experience every time someone else is baptized. The very sight of the open baptistery can have the same effect. But we can add in a more corporate dimension as we think of the many times the baptismal pool has been used. This will bring sadness as well as joy as we think of some who may have drifted away from their faith; it will call us to pray for them and for others who have moved on to other churches or spheres of work or ministry. It will prompt us to give thanks for the continuity of witness and life-changing response to the community. No doubt the same will be true for other traditions as they focus on the christening font, or the rail at which they kneel to receive communion. Now, the fact that such recollections and reflections will have gone on for us before, and do go on for many others who have not made our present journey, does not invalidate, but rather confirms, the processes we are encouraging. It shows that this kind of awareness is normal and valid, but we can also foster and enhance it, and learn to hear God more fully and clearly through the processes.

Obviously this sort of journey backwards in time can be experienced with any and all of the special features which surround us in our worship setting. They apply to the audible as well as the visible. Equally we can introduce touch and smell to enhance our awareness also. So, for me, when I receive the bread and wine in our Baptist way – a tiny, individual cup with a few drops of grape juice, and a small cube of bread placed clinically on the tiny aluminium plate which sits on the glass cup – I do not only eat. I hold the bread in my hand, I feel it, and sense it. God speaks many things to me then – not least that he has given himself over, in Christ, into the hands of sinful people who had the power to destroy and to crush the physical, but not to rob God of his achievements. I do not only drink, I smell the wine – the mixture of sweet and bitter, the message of which, although double, is also very clear: the bitterness of pain and death; the sweetness of forgiveness, life, and love. While, inevitably, this sounds very general it can often be a very special, specific, deep, and personal encounter with God – even before I eat and drink the elements and add in all the rich religious imagery, symbolism, and sacramental power of the service.

However, on another occasion I might visually explore the structure of that piece of bread. I might recall it was cut with a steel blade and remember the hardness of the nails which penetrated the hands with as little resistance as the bread offered. I will understand that this piece belongs to a whole from which it has been separated. I will see that this fragment of bread was made from wheat and yeast and water, elements gathered from different parts of the world – and I will experience the joy of knowing that Christ's living body incorporates people of many different kinds within our church, or people of many different nationalities within the worldwide Church – and I receive from them all and I am part

of them all. Or I may reflect that Christ's "body" had distinct
components – human and divine – just as the water and the wheat
are completely different kinds of realities, yet combined into one.
So investigating the structure can lead in various directions, each of
which can move me to thanksgiving, repentance, intercession, or
adoration. Through this God may speak a special word. Then,
when, on Monday morning, I come to put a piece of bread in the
toaster or cut the children's sandwiches for lunch, the realities I
have experienced in communion can be poured into my secular
moments. God comes, like a glint of sunshine from the cloudy sky,
into my daily life.

Yet our place of worship is not only a gift of "special" objects, it
is also full of very ordinary ones, like light bulbs or fluorescent
tubes as well as (maybe) candles; ordinary chairs as well as
(maybe) pews; carpet as well as kneelers. It has (hopefully) a
central heating system as well as a spiritually warm atmosphere.
It probably has a keyboard as well as an official pipe organ. It may
have dust on ledges as well as stained-glass windows or banners.
Why should we not bring our awareness of God in the everyday,
modern world to bear on the modern things in our worship centre?
God may choose to speak to us through these features of our
environment in church as well as in the city precinct. Again, we
have noted that sometimes it is not only "the thing" but "the thing"
"in contrast to" or "focused by" or "illuminated with" something or
someone else. So it may be the Scripture reading, or something the
preacher says, or the choir sings which "fits" with some feature
around us to which we have already given attention and we then
know God has spoken, or the truth penetrates more deeply because
we have brought our awareness of God in the world into our
worship.

The very fact that we are open to such possibilities will help to
dissolve the boundaries between Church and world, sacred and
secular in both directions, enriching our whole lives.

There is another subsidiary, yet potentially valuable, application.
Most of us find it easier to worship within a tradition and ethos
which corresponds to our personality, upbringing, and "personal
preference". It is not always easy for someone for whom order,
form, reverence, history, and tradition are helpful elements in
worship to feel at home with the apparent informality, vigour,
spontaneity, and personal emphasis of the House Church worship.
It is not easy for those who value action, involvement, and the
modern music of the black churches to find God in reflection,

quiet, and the classical. Those who normally worship at "the Friends" may find an Orthodox celebration is initially strange. The whole process may seem contrived and cluttered. Conversely, the Orthodox may find the Friends context and content mundane and even threadbare – a totally inappropriate expression for the glory and victory of the exalted Christ.

However, in two ways our journey of meditating in the modern world can help us cross the boundaries, and at least begin to find God in other styles and ways of worship. First, the very fact we have learnt that God can speak to us and meet with us in and through what, at first, seemed inappropriate ways and contexts, should help increase our sense that we can expect the unexpected. Indeed the approaches and avenues we have taken in our secular contemporary world may give us "handles" on traditions other than our own. In other words, we may be able to enter their riches and discover their value by a less direct route, utilizing the approaches we have tried in our secular world. After all, there are other ways to capture a walled city than by attacking the main gate with a frontal onslaught. Second, we may be able to begin by focusing on the ordinary features in the alien religious environment. Finding that God speaks to us through these here, may help us over-come our unfortunate, but understandable resistances, which are normally far deeper and more pervasive than the merely rational level of our being. So, again, our secular encounters with God may prove to be doorways to another kind of religious-based encounter.

BACK TO PEOPLE

We have investigated our modern world very largely as though it provided us with I–it relationships in this sense – that most of the realities which have helped us become more aware of God in our world have been objects, and even when people have been "used" they were in impersonal situations like "tube trains". However, our openness to the potential of objects to be the vehicle for God to meet with us, coupled with our willingness to become aware of the deeper significance of everything around us, is moving us constantly towards I–Thou relationships. This term, first expounded by Martin Buber, stands as shorthand for those relationships which involve deep respect for the other, a willing-ness, indeed a desire, to be responsive towards and receptive to other people, and so on. Martin Buber[1] used it to point to the very different qualities in truly personal relationships. He sees our relationship with God as fundamentally an I–Thou one, for we do not seek to use and dominate God but we seek for deep appreciation and understanding. These perceptions form the background for what follows. I sense that in five related ways our openness to God may help us be more fully human and may enable us to be more perceptive, receptive, and caring in our interactions.

First, we are, hopefully, going to be richer, deeper people because we are learning to live more consistently with God. People will sense and appreciate something special about us; there will be an enriched quality to our personhood because we are sensitized to, and by, God. The famous paradigm for this is Moses returning from a momentous (or should we say mountainous) encounter with God, during which he received the commandments.

> *When Moses went down from Mount Sinai carrying the Ten Commandments, his face was shining because he had been speaking with the Lord; but he did not know it. Aaron and all the people looked at Moses and saw that his face was shining, and they were afraid to go near him. But Moses called them, and Aaron and all the leaders of the community went to him, and Moses spoke to them. After that, all the people of Israel gathered round him, and Moses gave them all the laws that the Lord had given him on Mount Sinai. When Moses had finished speaking to them, he covered his face with a veil. Whenever Moses went into the Tent of the Lord's presence to speak to the Lord, he took the veil off. When he came out, he would tell the people of Israel everything that he had been commanded to say, and they would see that his face was shining.*

> Exodus 34.29–35a

The implication of this passage is that each time Moses encounters God "the shining" is enhanced and people sense the reflected glory. It is not without significance that the issues which had concerned God and Moses included very mundane ones – about harvest times, and which bread to bring to the sacrifice, and so on. As we encounter God through his world our being will be restored, however slightly, to its original glory.

Again, when Paul picks up this passage and develops it for the new covenant context he says:

> *All of us, then, reflect the glory of the Lord with uncovered*
> *faces; and that same glory, coming from the Lord, who is*
> *the Spirit, transforms us into his likeness in an ever greater*
> *degree of glory.*

2 Corinthians 3.18

The word translated "reflect" also means "gaze on" or "observe".
Glory, among its many facets, involves "showing forth the reality
which is normally hidden". So, the thought is that when we see
God's reality through Jesus Christ, this initiates a continuing
process of our being transformed into his glory, his likeness.

However, Paul goes on to say, "The God who said, 'Out of darkness the light shall shine!' is the same God who made his light
shine in our hearts, to bring us the knowledge of God's glory
shining in the face of Christ" (2 Corinthians 4.6). From our
perspective we can highlight the fact that the God who is at work in
Christ, transforming us through his Spirit, is also the God of
creation. For it is the creating God who said "Out of darkness the
light shall shine". As we become more aware of God in our world,
as we become more receptive to his encounter with us through our
environment, light will be shining out of the darkness and,
consciously or not, we shall reflect his glory to others. Putting it
simply, every relationship affects us. It is difficult to come away
from a boring conversation without having become tired and
listless. It is hard to leave a heated argument without a touch of
quarrelsomeness. It is difficult to live in a godless world without
communicating God's felt absence within ourselves to others. It is
equally difficult to live with an increased awareness of God, to
receive refreshing encounters with him, without carrying the marks
of this relationship to other people. Finding God through our
modern world will leave its mark on us – for God and for good.

So the first way in which uncovering God's presence in and
through our modern world helps us in our human relationships is
this. Through "hearing" God speak to us personally (which is
hopefully by now understood to be shorthand for becoming aware
of whatever God may be communicating to us through any of our
senses individually and in any combination) and responding so that
dialogue ensues, a divine quality will flow from us to other people.
This will in some way give them a sense of completion. That is,
they will feel that part of what has been missing from their lives
is being given to them. All of us need to be in touch with the
transcendent, and when we are, we shall communicate God's

qualities to others. However, it is also likely that if we bring a sense of God's presence with us it will also awaken and deepen the stirrings in other people for God's reality. A parallel in human terms would be if we are eating a bag of chips, then the "fragrance" is likely to generate a desire for them in other people we meet at that time! So, the second way in which we will contribute to others is to very gently and imperceptibly start to create in them a desire for God in their world and their experience. If our Christian view of human beings is correct, this is simultaneously to move them towards greater human fulfilment and reality. Sometimes this may be claiming too much for ourselves. However, at least we will be opening them up for God to slip into their lives.

A third contribution that living with a greater sense of God's presence in our world will make is through the process and skills with which we are becoming familiar. We are learning to "listen" with much more of our total being. We are learning to integrate the messages, the meaning, the significance of many different forms of information. We are discovering that we have collected many more kinds of stimuli from the environment around us, even the apparently inhuman environment. Through this we are becoming much more sensitized listeners. We are refusing to be stopped by the apparently uncooperative and non-communicating elements in our world. Inevitably we shall become better listeners for and to others. We shall "hear" things from other people; messages they would hardly dare to speak out for fear of rejection or misunderstanding; messages they will barely have heard themselves. When we begin to respond to these hints with love and sympathy they will be affirmed and encouraged to own their own cries of pain, suppressed joys, and whispered hopes. We will help them discover something of their deeper selves. In other words, we shall become better friends, bringing into our relationships both a greater awareness of stimuli given out by others, and a more sensitive capacity to unscramble the messages and make sense of them.

Allied with this we may discover an ability to "hear" what God is saying to others about their situations. This may happen in two ways which can be differentiated but, ultimately, not separated. First, because we are more able to listen to God through our technological world we may be able to discern what he is saying to *us* about them and for them. God may not only speak to us about ourselves, he may want to speak to us about other people. Not only our capacity to hear God, but also our confidence that he does communicate, will be significant here – for, if we are not open to the possibility of his meeting us and if we have not become comfortable with this process by experiencing the validation of our "encounters" as events have unfolded, we are unlikely to take the risk of relaying to others what we understand God has in mind for other people.

We will also realize that one reason he may be entrusting his message to us, rather than directly to them, is that he can get through to us and not them. If, when I am away from home, and for some reason I cannot get through to my family on the phone (maybe because the phone has become unplugged), then I would contact a neighbour or friend and ask them to call round and deliver my message for them. This would not only get my message through, but also alert the family to check the phone. Thus in the long run it would restore the possibility of a dialogue of a more personal nature. Similarly, God may choose to deliver his message to others through us because our communication system is operative and for some reason he can get through to us more conveniently than to them. As with the telephone, we may not only carry God's message to them but also alert them to check their system. The fact that I want to speak to my family and am able to do so because I am at the other end of a phone is a motivational factor for them to get their phone in order. So for our friends, the astounding fact that God may be wanting to speak to them may itself motivate them to learn to listen more. There are many other reasons why God may choose to speak to our friends through us. It may be more to do with our needs than our sensitivities, so there is no room for pride here! Nor is there any room for dogmatism in conveying the message. We can always get it wrong!

The second angle on this issue is that we may discern what God is saying to them when they are unable to hear the indicators. To follow on the telephone analogy – sometimes when I am at home my daughter hears the phone ringing and takes the message for me. This is partly because her hearing is more acute than mine, partly because of her greater and more hopeful expectations that the phone will ring. Just as there are a variety of responses to the situation with the phone, so there are when we think we are hearing God speak to people through their world. With the phone, not only can my daughter take the message but she could call me to the phone, or carry messages from me to the person ringing in. She might also say, "Dad, the phone's ringing", thus awakening me to the possibility that someone wants to get through. The parallels with us recognizing God seeking to reach others through their world will be obvious – although be warned it won't always be obvious what the most helpful procedure for our friends will be. What is vitally important is that we convey our perceptions of what God is saying to others with a deep humility (we can easily be wrong – he may be speaking to us and we don't want to hear it for ourselves etc.), and also with the desire to get out of the way and not set ourselves up as indispensable mediators.

When we move from hearing our friends better because of more sensitized listening skills, to hearing what God is saying to our friends through our awareness of his presence in the world, we are moving into an area of Christian counselling. It is important to be aware of all the boundaries like confidentiality and all the safeguards, such as not imposing solutions to people's problems, which need to operate in this area. Nevertheless, we cannot and should not exclude the possibility of God communicating in this way. Christian counselling is essentially a development of ordinary human friendship, but without proper training it is probably better to recognize that people need to seek for qualified and specialized help, and be willing to refer people on to the appropriate sources.

The fourth way in which our increased awareness of God's desire to meet with us can work is also a development of the friendship relationship. Rather than lead in the direction of counselling this time it leans towards evangelism. Haenchey has written a fascinating book called *Church Growth and the Power of Evangelism* (Cambridge, Massachusetts, 1990). The title doesn't really help us make the connection so let me explain briefly what is the book's special contribution. Starting from the premise that God is at work in our lives the author seeks to sensitize us to God's presence. "Coincidences" should not be dismissed first of all, but rather investigated for the indications that God is doing something. Often we will find that looking at our lives this way makes more sense of what is really happening to us through apparently unconnected events and, as a significant bonus, helps us appreciate the livingness of God's relationship with us. We are then encouraged to take the insight from our own experience and help others investigate their lives, discovering for themselves the possibility of God moving in and with, their life experience.

In a similar way, I believe, we can help people make the connection between things, events, and perceptions, and the possibility that God is moving into their lives. In other words, we can use our experience of how God can speak to us through our world to illuminate the same reality for other people in their (basically similar) world. The God and Father of our Lord Jesus Christ is a God who comes to seek and save the lost. When Jesus told his parables he was directing people to the possibility of God in their world as well as his. Obviously, it will also be appropriate with some people to share our stories as to how we are finding God meets with us in our world. Thus our own discovery will become part of our overall testimony. For some "unbelievers" this will be a very powerful testimony as one of their major barriers will be a sense (often unfocused) that our modern world has made it impossible to believe in God. We shall be presenting them with the opposite claim: the truth that, through our world, God is frequently speaking to us – and by implication is able to do so to them. But, because we will be admitting this was something we had previously overlooked, we may well encourage them to reconsider its possibility for them as well. As there is considerable evidence that many "unbelievers" have some significant experiences of transcendence, but either cannot interpret it, or acknowledge it for themselves or to others, our conversations with them may provide the necessary categories or courage to own their experiences. They may also realize that as we have started the process of discovery ourselves, we may be in a good position to help them too. So, in these two related ways, our journey can have a distinctively evangelistic potential.

BACK TO GOD

Our greater alertness to God through our synthetic world can bring new dimensions into the "religious world" and the "relational world". It is not something that can or should be kept in a water-tight compartment. Indeed it is important we don't try to do so, but rather do our utmost to cause it to spill over into every part of life. Our starting point was a desire (from our point of view) to let God back into all our living, and not keep him for the beautiful and rustic in terms of meditation. We perceived that there are some dangers if we confine the focus of our meditations to such aspects of life. So it would be ironic if, having developed a facility for receiving from God through the normal everyday modern world, we segregated this from the rest of life, including the contexts in which we worship corporately, and the communities large and small to which we belong.

It would be ironic in the extreme if we started to isolate our new-found awareness from other ways of relating to God, or indeed started to claim it is the only valid way for people to have a relationship with God at the end of this century. To do this would not only be to isolate but would also be to idolize one approach. Because I am aware that this kind of idolatry is a constant tendency for people, I want to give some brief thought to the issue of integration. The approaches of this book need to be part of a more comprehensive and holistic understanding of our relationship with God. We have already done this in part by giving a biblical basis for what we are attempting and by affirming the value of other styles of meditation. But I want to do more now, and recommend other approaches to "spirituality" as valid and necessary. God is not confined in any sense, shape, or form to our technological, consumer-orientated world. Nor are the insights we may gain to be evaluated as more relevant or more right. I have been writing about impact level rather than revelation level. I have been seeking to open up possibilities of immediacy rather than making claims for superiority. My task has been a parallel to that of a modern sculptor who tries to indicate that a message can be conveyed through modern materials as well as clay and bronze, and through modern forms as well as the more traditional ones. I believe that establishing the possibility and feasibility of this is vitally important to help us be at home in our world and to be more human in it, but God forbid we should in any way discard the wealth of the past.

Coventry is my home and so on many occasions I have the opportunity to visit Coventry Cathedral. There are a multitude of significant and moving aspects to this cathedral, dominated by Sutherland's tapestry of the glorified and ascended Christ. One of the small features typifies some aspects of what I mean. On a wall near to the Chapel of Unity is a small sculpture of a human head. The casual visitor, if they give it only a glance as they stride towards the chapel, might wonder what it was doing there because, superficially, it appears to be a configuration and conflagration of scrap metal. More careful attention reveals that it is far more – the mangled metal conveys a human face and head. Reading the inscription reveals why. It was given in memory of a young person by that person's parents. The young person was killed in a car crash which set the car on fire. The scrap metal from the car has been used for the sculpture. There are all kinds of levels of meaning given with and through this sculpture: the destructive power of modern technology; the contrast between a real living face of a human being and the mangled mess to which they have been reduced through the car. But there are also many positive ones – the refusal to let the destructive darkness of a vicious accident rob people of the human being they have borne, nurtured, and loved; the sense that in God's house, especially this one where forgiveness has been burnt into the fabric of the place and from which the message of God's power of reconciliation and redemption still flows, is where the chaos and threat of our modern world can be handled, and given releasing and healing significance. Why precisely this sculpture was given to the cathedral and placed where it is, I do not know, but for me it is a symbol that all technology and negativity has a place within the hands of a crucified, risen, and ascended Lord. Many people will be challenged to bring their "wreck" and surrender it; many will be comforted in their confusion that God can make something of viciously damaged lives. God can speak through our modern world, and does.

However, there are other cathedrals that I also visit and from the sublime architecture and older traditions I can also receive other messages from God and receive aspects of meaning for my life, and a sense of purpose for the world. In their quietness, I can glimpse a glory and holiness that is different from the sense of God I gain in Coventry. I am aware of a stability and continuity which Coventry cannot give. In a similar way other aspects of spirituality can be my openings into heaven. They, too, can amplify God's voice into my heart. So all I am commending, necessary and vital as I consider it to be, is no replacement for other approaches, whether that be through group Bible study and prayer, personal devotion, social action, the discipline of fasting, the liturgy of the Church, the openness to God's Spirit touching our spirit, the exuberance of pentecostalism or the commitment of South American base communities. Nor is it to be understood to encourage a retreat from worshipping with, and commitment to, the people of God. Indeed I would hope that the kind of approach we have been investigating will be used by groups and worshipping communities as well as by individuals, just as is the case with other forms of meditation. Neither am I in any way wishing to suggest that God's revelation of himself in Christ, mediated to us now through Scripture, is in anything but primary and absolute. Take Scripture away and I for one would expect to be completely lost. But although it is true that there is no substitute for knowing someone personally, it is also true that letter, phone, fax, and electronic mail can be useful means of communication. We may need to know the person before we can be sure of the authenticity of the other forms and, perhaps more pertinent to our present concerns, before we can give the right nuances and interpretations to the messages we are receiving through modern technology, but they can still tell us a great deal we would not know without them. It is similar for the kind of approach to meditation we are developing. In this analogy Scripture, as the primary source of revelation, can be considered the equivalent to the personal meetings, and our approach to meditating in the contemporary world equates to the telephone and fax. So this approach is to be seen as a valid and appropriate supplement, and not a substitute either for biblical revelation, community participation, or other forms of spirituality. They can all enrich one another, but without the sensitivity to God in our everyday world there is the danger of implying that God does not belong here at the turn of the millennium.

There is one other comment that I wish to make about spirituality and the approach I am recommending. It is this: the same rules apply. Scripture teaches us that our relationship with God is no longer our right, it is an enormous privilege, only feasible because Christ, through his death on the cross, his resurrection, and exaltation, has opened up for us a new and living way. The privilege of hearing God in our world depends on this historical event of eternal significance. Without salvation there would be no relationship to enjoy and foster. Scripture also teaches us that the quality of this continuing relationship for the believer is affected by our responses to God and our relations with others. The same rules apply. If we are deliberately disobedient to the things God is saying to us, we shall find it harder to hear him, whichever approach we are using. Confession and receiving forgiveness are still necessary. Scripture shows us that if we start to trivialize or tamper with the truth of God then our receptivity will degenerate or God will withdraw – the same rules apply. Scripture teaches us that if we seek God with all our heart we shall surely find him – if we are not willing to make God our priority and give him quality time, it is unlikely (although God is in my experience infinitely gracious) that we shall keep our receptivity to him; that applies in this realm as much as anywhere.

So we could go on but I hope the point is understood. What we are attempting together is not some gimmicky technique, it is about ultimate reality, and God in his mercy and love remains consistent in the conditions for our relationship with him. This is not because he is either a tyrant or finicky but because he is God and we are made in his image, even though fallen, and so for our relationship to be valid it has to be the way he prescribes.

Nevertheless, our ability to "find God" in and through the events and features of late twentieth-century life is something which can make an important contribution to the fullness of our relationship with God as well as with other people. It can help us in our world of worship as well as our world of work. Not to venture into the rich experiences which technology and modernity offer, is to fail to recognize that God is with us.

Suggested Activities

1. One valid criticism which can be made of this chapter is that it presents an individualistic approach to worship. For those who have used this book in a group context an important issue is how the experiences you value, which have come to you corporately, can be transferred into the more normal worship context. Please spend time sharing insights on this issue.

2. How does viewing people as "made in God's image" affect the way we relate to each other? Does it alter the way we appreciate people's achievements? Has this introduction to meditating in our modern world helped or hindered your perception of God's image in others? Why not keep a notebook/diary in which to log your perceptions?

3. Try to list five truths about God which you have come to appreciate either for the first time or in a more immediate way through the approach to meditation which this book suggests. Then give thanks to God for what you have discovered about him, and ask him to help you integrate the truths of who he is into your lifestyle.

Notes
1. Martin Buber, *I and Thou*, Whitakers (1968)

15 CONCLUSION

I anticipate there will be three kinds of people reading this final chapter and I would like it to assist each of them. First, there will be those who are wondering *whether to make an investment in the book*, either by buying it, borrowing it from the library, or by reading it. Like me, they often turn to the back of a book first! For them there is a very brief summary of the approach and applications made in this book. A more comprehensive summary will be found at the beginning of Chapter 13. Such people may well find skimming through the rest of that chapter helpful too, because it is especially for people who have very little free personal time but who sense the need to add a quality element to their pressurized existence.

Second there will be those who have simply read through the book much as they would try to read any other book, like a novel or autobiography. In your case the fact that you have come this far suggests that you have found it interesting or have been intrigued by the plot. I am delighted. Perhaps at this stage in your life development that may be enough and maybe at some later point, an experience you go through or a need you are aware of, will trigger memories and you will recall what you have read and choose to revisit it. However, the fact that you have kept reading to the end may well indicate that you are ready to benefit from this book in a more significant way. Let's reflect on this point. It is possible to read a book of poems or a "Teach Yourself German" book as we read a novel. Doing so will communicate something. But not all books are at their best read as we read novels. This is one of those books. With a book of poetry, for instance, it is often best to go to the poem which has appealed to us and spend time with that one. There will be several reasons any poem attracts us – the subject, the layout, the length, a vivid image etc. We may not be very aware of what the reasons are. But as we revisit a particular poem we find our understanding and appreciation of the poem develops, and we can move on to other poems gradually gaining insight into and empathy with the poet, so in the end we can enjoy and be enriched by nearly all the poems. In the process we may discover that "our favourite" is no longer our initial entrance poem but another. Similarly, with this book, why not go back to a chapter or even a particular illustrative subject and spend more time with it? Then, as you gain confidence and understand that this is not only an interesting book to read but also one key to developing your relationship with God, you will be able to identify with more and more of the book, and make its insights your own.

This book does not have to be read and used sequentially. Here, it is helpful to think in terms of a book which helps us to learn a new language. It is only by doing the exercises that we begin to grasp the meaning in a fuller way. Of course, having to do the exercises slows us up, but it deepens and broadens comprehension, leading to a greater satisfaction. For many the same will apply to this book. If you have found it interesting why not now try and apply the insights and methods for yourself? It may seem an interruption, it may feel like hard work, but it will add enormously to the value of this book in your life experience, and quite soon it will lead to a higher appreciation of the book and, what is far more important, to a deeper awareness of God.

The third kind of reader will be the one for whom the approaches of this book have now become part of life's normal routine, almost as natural as breathing. By now you hardly need the book, except to pass on to a friend to help them into something of the riches you have found that lie all around you in the ordinary modern world. For you, reading this last chapter is almost unnecessary but it is a "kind of proper thing to do", like putting in the full stop at the end of the sentence!

For you I have tried to gather together a few questions that have drifted up into my mind over the last two or three years concerning this kind of approach. I have also shared my response to the questions, although please do not think that I have said the last word on any of them. I certainly don't think this, at all. Maybe God has spoken with you about them!

SUMMARY

We began with Scriptures which speak movingly of the presence of God and then faced what is reality for many of us, that God does not seem present in our everyday modern world. We affirmed the value of Christian Meditation but realized that its focus is on the quiet, the rural, and the romantic, rather than what is for many their real world today. We looked at some of the roots of this approach and began to sense that Scripture did not encourage us to stay with this kind of focus.

I then shared some key stages on my own spiritual journey, including the "discovery" of imaginative Bible studies, Christian

Meditation, and the value of shared experiences in this area. For me, Scripture is primary. Therefore we looked next at aspects of God's presence in our world, as represented throughout Scripture. We also found that from a theological perspective as well as from particular examples, Scripture encourages us to expect that God will meet with us in the ordinary everyday world around us.

This section then looked at some of the factors involved in hearing from God through our world. We found Bill Hybel's story of his friend's mobile phone helpful in elucidating key points. We believed the attempt to hear from God was one worth bothering about because it is necessary if we are going to cope spiritually in our contemporary culture and if we are to develop fully rounded Christian personalities.

We were then ready for the second main section of the book, in which we moved from more theoretical considerations to the more practical ones of how we can grow in our awareness of God in our world. We began with the more familiar aspects of Christian Meditation. Then, using a very ordinary domestic event – peeling potatoes – I unpacked the fact that interwoven with such apparently trivial happenings are a multiplicity of particularities and valid significancies, for which science is not really an appropriate method of understanding. So much of reality is missed, unless we stop and search.

Next came a "listening" experiment to show that the same is true in terms of our awareness of all the messages our senses are giving us. This experience is a parable for learning to listen to God. It is not that we need to imagine he is there or invent his message – we need to become aware of what he is seeking to share with us. In a similar way we made use of a visual focus – a candle – and some tactile ones.

It was then time to move further away from traditional territory. Our next chapters moved us on using artistic ability and imagination to interact with the world, then through looking with a new openness, whether in the gutter or the windows, at everyday objects, but also, surely appropriate for our modern world, the view from a motorway bridge. From the outer world we began to look into the modern world, to see under the bonnet of a motor car and hear what God might say. Then we took an electrical plug in our hands and wondered how it might speak for God as we examined it. Chapter 9 capitalized on the power of objects to open up our memories. We recognized that some of these will bring us pain – Christmas lights are a case in point for me.

A very different set of associations came with an iron and a vase. We then took a cornflakes packet and its content. Using this focus we travelled the world and allowed God to speak to us through it. Next we recalled that our modern world involves visits. The visit to the dentist and the supermarket are different in many respects but both can lead us to encounter God's perspective on our lives and both can be opportunities for discovering God's relevance to our lives. Following this we picked up on some of the sounds of our world, then touch and smell were explored a little too. The last chapter of this section took account of the rush of our world, and discovered what using keys and waiting for a lift could contribute, as well as suggesting several other moments that could be made meaningful by sensing God's message in them.

In all of this we have sought not only to hear God through common objects and experiences of our everyday world, but also to educate all our faculties and integrate them into the process of sensitizing us to God's presence. Enriched with all of this we returned to three fundamental arenas, those of our place of worship, our relationship with others, and with God.

Undoubtedly the range of awareness covered by this book is wide, and to gain from the whole spectrum is demanding – but for me it is immensely worth while and necessary.

Our final few pages focus on some questions which the whole process poses for us.

SOME QUESTIONS FOR FURTHER REFLECTION

Human imaginings or divine insight

One of the questions which probes my mind, and perhaps yours, too, is "Is all of this simply my imagination or is it really insight from, and conversation with God?" This is an important matter. Sometimes this question comes drifting along. At first I am not sure I have noted it, then gradually stronger and stronger, like the smell of the cake overcooking in the oven, it grips me. Eventually it impacts my awareness so powerfully, so that I have to do something about it or there will be a disaster. Sometimes the question is much more probing and demanding like the stab of toothache.

In Genesis 3.1 the snake says to Eve, "Has God really said…?" If the approach this book suggests is one way God loves to commune with his children, then it is dangerous to ignore the opportunity and refuse his gift of love, as dangerous as it was for Baalam to decide his ass was being awkward and stupid (Numbers 22). However, if it is only our human imagination, then, we are in danger of breaking

one of the primary commandments not to make false gods: we can
do this as effectively with our imaginations as with our hands. I have
no wish or intention to be selling idols with my book! How can we
get a grip on this very slippery question?

First we need to see if we can establish in our minds the feasibility
and possibility that God may communicate with us personally, and
may do it through the world around us. In the light of our belief in
God as Father, Creator, and the Incarnate One it seems to be a very
reasonable feasibility. As Father, he would want to establish regular
communication through his world, even the ordinary things, as any
human father would. As Creator, he has the authority to use anything
for his purposes (and as redeemer he can claim back anything and
recycle it for his purposes). As Creator he also has the wisdom to
realize its potential in this way. As the Incarnate One he has indicated
his willingness to involve himself and express himself through all the
messiness of ordinary human existence. So it seems feasible that God
may communicate with us in this way. The details of Scripture press
us to conclude that it is also possible. Time and time again Scripture
shows that God speaks through everyday objects as well as the
unusual, through secular happenings as well as sacred services, in
mundane circumstances as well as religious places. Further, Scripture
shows us that God uses the more imaginative side of our nature as a
partner in this process – dreams, poetry, music, imagery, story, and
parable are all indicators of this, as is the constant appeal to memory,
the importance of tradition, and the use of sacraments. So God clearly
does not restrict his communication process to the rational track alone.

So, it seems we can establish the feasibility and possibility that
God may speak to us through the kinds of meditative openings we
have suggested.

However, there are two other issues to unwrap. The first is, who
should do the initiating? Most scriptural examples which come
to mind suggest that God begins the "conversation": whether it is
Joseph's dreams or Peter's, whether it is Jeremiah's underwear,
or Jeroboam's cloak, whether it is a New Testament catch of fish or
an Old Testament fish's catch (Genesis 37.3–11; Acts 10.9–16;
Jeremiah 13.1–11; 1 Kings 11.29–39; Luke 5.4–11; Jonah 1.12–17).

Scripture also indicates that it is wrong to try and manipulate or
compel God to speak, for this implies a fundamental failure to understand and appreciate God's sovereignty. Yet Scripture is full of
counter-indications. God invites us to seek him and promises that if
we do seek him we shall find him. God appeals often to his people to
listen to him and, sometimes, with a deeply sorrowful heart, laments

the fact that although he has sought our attention in many ways we have refused to respond. This affirms for me the validity of our desire to open up as many parts of our lives and environments as possible, so they can become a means of two-way communication with God. Naturally the same conditions for relating to God apply here as in any other approach to him, honesty, humility, a desire for holiness etc. But in no way does God say "Wait for me, don't you dare come looking for me, who do you think you are?" Further, the approach we are investigating does not rule out proper humility. Our prayer can be "Lord, show me, how, where, and when you want me, direct me to the things you want to use to reach me – you know best".

The final consideration is how we can know that what we think we experience and perceive really is from God. Here, the difficulties are no different to other ways we accept that God may communicate with us. If it is through prayer – how do we know it is not our own thoughts; if it is through a preacher how do we know it is not our own suggestibility, through guilt, for instance, or our openness because we like him or her, or our over-compensation because we don't? If it is through reading Scripture, how do we know that, in general, it is not our interpretation and, in particular, that this specific verse is the one God really wants us to pay attention to?

The question might appear to imply the answer "We can't know", but in practice we know we can grow in our spiritual sensitivity and integrity, for we are not alone. The Holy Spirit is within us and he bears witness with our spirit when God's truth is reaching us. However there is no reason why the Holy Spirit will not do so with equal measure along the pathways we are considering at the moment.

Fortunately there is a vital litmus test which may rule out the possibility that our awareness is from God – namely if the character of God to which it relates, or the direction it gives to our lives is out of step with Scripture. A further check comes by sharing our insights with Christian people we trust. We are safer "in fellowship"; it is together we have the mind of Christ. Here too we can bring in the value of Christian tradition because this is a form of fellowship with "all the saints".

Nevertheless, even when we are satisfied that our experience with God through our modern world is compatible with God as we know him in Christ revealed in Scripture, it could be argued that we still cannot be sure that "this" is his word for us now. While this is true, it is not so constrictive as we might at first think. Why? Because if it is God's truth anyway there is no harm in responding to it. Moreover, if it is the kind of insight which leads to actions, say, helping our neighbour, or asking forgiveness of a family member, we can proceed to explore the situation, taking small steps one at a time. We can cover the whole process in prayer and affirm our promise to God that we will follow through on his will, as he makes the route clear. Finally, even if we have got it wrong, God still approves of our attempt, and will foster and encourage our ability to recognize him through the contemporary world.[1]

Meditation and spiritual gifts

My second question is as follows, "What is the relationship, if any, between the kind of approach to meditation we have developed and the spiritual gifts such as the gift of wisdom, knowledge, and discernment or even prophecy?"

The first conclusion I reach is that we must not confuse this or any other approach to God with the spiritual gifts he may choose to give. So, this means that all of us are free to seek for God using the methods and insights indicated in this book. In so doing we are not seeking to force his hand in any way. We have attempted to keep a balance between God's sovereignty – hence his freedom to meet with us or not – and his fatherhood, which implies his desire to communicate frequently with his children. Equally, we preserve, I trust, proper respect for his freedom. Scripture expresses it this way: "as he wishes, he gives a different gift to each person" (1 Corinthians 12.11).

Nevertheless gifts from God need to be developed and deployed; we are not to neglect them. Many of our scriptural examples of God speaking through the world around us show that prophets often glimpsed God's message in this kind of way. So those who find a particular facility in this approach, who discover great relevance, deep immediacy, frequent encounter etc., may well be people whom God is gifting along this axis, which leads to some form of insight beyond that which is available normally to all Christians.

If people sense this to be the case, they need to take the same kind of care in developing and using such gifts as they would any other spiritual gift. They need to develop it with the same due reverence and responsibility if their awareness of the gift comes through the journey of this book as if it had come to them by any other route.

In short, I am prayerfully hoping that using this book may enlarge the gifting of God for his Church in this area, but I also hope a much wider range of Christian people will benefit from it.

When God seems absent

My final question is this, "What if I never seem to make any contact with God this way?" Such a question prods into my pastoral heart! I am aware of a fear within me that in writing this book I am raising people's expectations and they will go away with a greater sense of failure, their hunger will be more intense etc. Let me assure you first that if this book hasn't helped you build your relationship with God it could well have much more to do with my inadequacies than from any issue within you.

However, I would like to comment on one or two points the question raises.

First, it may not be a helpful method for you, for a variety of reasons. It may be something to do with personality types, it may be that God is speaking to you in such a pertinent and direct way through the Scriptures that this method seems to be a distraction for you. It may be that at this time, because of some life crisis, or transition experience, it is not appropriate. Often at times such as a bereavement, it seems as though our whole being is numbed, in some cases for several years. So no matter what approach we try, however much we long for an awareness of God's love in our lives, there seems nothing, nothing at all.

Clearly, people who are in that kind of situation are all the more likely to turn to books like this to give them the help they need. If this is your position, I would quietly ask you neither to condemn yourself nor the book. Put it away for the new day, when you sense a new spring returning to your spiritual self and then God may prompt you to use it, and you may well find that it is the kind of tool which truly helps. Try also neither to despise as naïve, nor envy, those who find the book helps. Hard as it will be, try to thank God, even if he doesn't seem to be there, that others are being helped.

Second, I am beginning to sense that people approach books with two different mind sets. In the first case, a book will help people move into a situation, understand an issue, learn an aspect of truth. The book will actually take them along into a new experience. Such people learn forwards through books. Other people learn through books backwards. In other words the book will help them explore and explain mental territory that they have passed through, normally recently, but sometimes a long while ago. It may be that you are the kind of person for whom books are a help mainly to learn backwards. So the reason this book is not helping you, is that you need some current and vivid experiences, which will help you penetrate and claim the book's truth. You need experiences to help you understand the book and then benefit from its other suggestions. What I would recommend in this case is that you try and find other people who can identify with the approach of this book and that you ask God to surprise you with the kind of insight and encounter mentioned in it. Then, when you have built up at least a small bank of experience, return to the book and try again, to see if, armed as you now are with the light of experience, you can interact with it.

In writing this way, I may already have prompted some memories, which are now beginning to float to the surface. Memories of glimpses of God in and through the world around us, that we have dismissed, or so to speak put in the wastepaper bin like unopened post, because we had not perceived their value. In this case a relaxed time of re-evaluation may provide all the bank-balance of experience we need.

Having said all this, I am aware that some people may not find the approach helpful, because of traumatic, bad experiences, because of blocks on their receptivity due to critical words about those who stray from "the Book", or even because they are choosing to live out of relationship with God through deliberate sin. Indeed, it is possible that some may be attracted to this way, who have never realized that any kind of relationship with God is a gift not a right. It is a gift which comes to us through the unmerited generosity of God. We are all sinners, that is, people who have broken off our relationship with God, through our witting or unwitting disobedience. The only way for us to have any contact with God is through accepting that the price for restoration has been paid by Jesus Christ, when he died on the cross. We need to repent, that is, completely change our minds about who God is, about what we are, and about the way to God. Without this there can be no justifiable expectation that God can or will reach us.

For any of the situations mentioned in the previous paragraph, I would suggest contacting a Christian counselling service[2] or, if you have one, a trusted, mature Christian friend or church leader. This is not a situation of despair! It implies that God wants to help us and can do so, but that he makes his loving and healing help available through his people.

God is a very wonderful God, and we live in a wonderful world, which is his creation. Our world is no alien place for God, he has made it his home and today as at any other time, he can come to meet us in and through it. There is a special joy and a definite strength when we discover for ourselves that God is around us in our world. It is a discovery we need for ourselves as we pioneer towards the next millennium – God will not be left behind. It is discovery we need for many of our friends whose image of God is like a relic from a past, a forgotten, dusty generation. It is a discovery God is longing for us to make.

> *For this reason we have always prayed for you, ever since we heard about you. We ask God to fill you with the knowledge of his will, with all the wisdom and understanding that his Spirit gives. Then you will be able to live as the Lord wants and will always do what pleases him. Your lives will produce all kinds of good deeds, and you will grow in your knowledge of God.*

Colossians 1.9–11

> *In conclusion, my brothers and sisters, fill your minds with those things that are good and that deserve praise: things that are true, noble, right, pure, lovely, and honourable. Put into practice what you learnt and received from me, both from my words and from my actions. And the God who gives you peace will be with you.*

Philippians 4.8–9

> *And God's peace, which is far beyond human understanding, will keep your hearts and minds safe in union with Christ Jesus.*

Philippians 4.7

Notes

1. Insights from books on God's guidance and discovering the will of God are useful in helping to provide us with a framework for evaluating our particular kinds of meditation. Among those I would recommend are W. E. Sangster, *God Does Guide Us* (London, 1934); G. Sweeting, *How to Discover the Will of God* (Chicago, 1975); D. Cleave, *How to Know God's Will* (Welwyn, 1985).

2. If there is no such service available to you, please write to either the Christian Enquiry Agency (Interchurch House, 35 Lower Marsh, London SE1 7RL) or Contact for Christ (Selsdon House, 212 Addington Road, Selsdon, South Croydon, Surrey CR2 8LD).